# Leonard C. Hawes
The Ohio State University

# Pragmatics of Analoguing: Theory and Model Construction in Communication

**Addison-Wesley Publishing Company**
Reading, Massachusetts · Menlo Park, California
London · Amsterdam · Don Mills, Ontario · Sydney

This book is in the
**Addison-Wesley Series in
Human Communication**

Consulting Editor
C. David Mortensen

ISBN 0-201-02822-0
ABCDEFGHIJ-DO-798765

*To Laina and John*

# Foreword

Society is often described as an ongoing system of communication maintained by persons committed to the principle of consistent action. Similarly, this series in Human Communication is designed to explore the ongoing and pervasive impact of communication on the actions and patterns of everyday experience. The series provides a flexible and integrated discussion of key concepts, problems, topics, and issues related to "person-centered" subject matter. The books strive to be readable, nontechnical, and broadly based without sacrificing the depth needed to challenge serious students.

In developing such an important collection of texts, Addison-Wesley has called upon a well-known group of teachers whose competence is ideally suited to their texts. *Communication Inquiry: A Perspective on a Process* by Gerald R. Miller and Henry E. Nicholson introduces students to various ways of studying communicative behavior as an integral dimension of personal and social experience. *Dyadic Communication: A Transactional Perspective* by William W. Wilmot focuses on the complex and fascinating processes that shape the experience of communication in interpersonal social situations. *Communication and Social Influence* by Stephen W. King broadens the study of communication to the context of what is known about the potentials and hazards of using language to influence and persuade others. An overview of language and speech as communication codes, within and between individuals, is the subject of Larry Wilder's *Speech, Language, and Communication* (forthcoming). The larger theoretical aspects of human communication are examined in *Pragmatics of Analoguing: Theory and Model Construction in Communication* by Leonard C. Hawes and in *Perspectives on Communication Theory* by Jesse G. Delia (forthcoming). *Pragmatics of Analoguing* provides the first systematic treatment of the requirements of developing theories about the underlying nature of communicative experience. Delia's text will complement other books in the series by providing a broadly based synthesis of recent contributions to the study of communication theory.

These brief, integrated paperback texts are suitable for a wide range of purposes and courses within communication and the social sciences. Used in combination or alone with other texts and supplements, they will enhance and enrich the study of human communication.

C. David Mortensen

# Preface

In his essay on "Imperfections of Science," Warren Weaver (1963) quotes the following lines from an e. e. cummings poem;

> (While you and i have lips and voices which
> are for kissing and to sing with
> who cares if some oneeyed son of a bitch
> invents an instrument to measure Spring with?

With a characteristic economy of words, cummings manages to question the anatomical normalcy of scientists, cast aspersions on their ancestors, and highlight a chasm supposedly separating C. P. Snow's two cultures; that of the scientist on the one hand and the humanist on the other.

In the case of communication, according to cummings's line of thinking, the humanist would be interested in exploring the communion and community dimensions of human relationships made possible through communication. The scientist, groping as best he could with limited vision and guilt-ridden about his origins, would invent an instrument to measure the meaning of words.

Are these characterizations of the humanist and scientist accurate? What are the similarities and differences between the two cultures in terms of the work they do? Why are an increasing number of communication scholars studying communicative behavior scientifically? What do they hope to gain from such activity? What kind of activity does a social scientist engage in to build theories and models?

This book was written to provide advanced undergraduate and graduate students with a set of answers to their questions. The book does not pretend to answer the questions in an exhaustive fashion; it claims only to offer the student some intellectual tools with which to pursue more thorough answers independently. The answers outlined in the following pages are not the only ones to these questions. There are several clearly defined philosophies of social science and each takes a slightly different position with respect to many of the issues surfaced.

Regardless of how completely you agree with the positions taken, however, my main objective is to demonstrate that doing social science research is an exhilarating intellectual experience. Far too many students unfamiliar (and many who are familiar) with the social and behavioral sciences equate such research with meticulous experimental designs, an awesome array of statistical tools, and extremely conservative conclusions. Certainly asking questions carefully, knowing appropriate means of answering questions, and resisting the temptation to generalize results irresponsibly are *necessary* conditions for doing social science. But they are not *sufficient* conditions. Care and rigor are pointless if the questions being asked lack imagination, insight, and intellectual relevance.

As the title of the book indicates, developing analogues lies at the heart of the social scientist's activity. An analogue (or analogy) is the use of a familiar object or idea to understand more completely an unfamiliar object or idea. Hesse (1966) uses the following example from physics.

> When we take a collection of billiard balls in random motion as a model for a gas, we are not asserting that billiard balls are in all respects like gas particles, for billiard balls are red or white, and hard and shiny, and we are not intending to suggest that gas molecules have these properties. We are in fact saying that gas molecules are *analogous* to billiard balls, and the relation of analogy means that there are some properties of billiard balls which are not found in molecules. Let us call those properties we know belong to billiard balls and not to molecules the *negative analogy* of the model. Motion and impact, on the other hand, are just the properties of billiard balls that we do want to ascribe to molecules in our model, and these we can call the *positive analogy*. Now the important thing about this kind of

model-thinking in science is that there will generally be some properties of the model about which we do not yet know whether they are positive or negative analogies; these are the interesting properties, because, as I shall argue, they allow us to make new predictions. Let us call this third set of properties the *neutral analogy* (p. 8).

The word *Analoguing* rather than *Analogues* is used in the title of the book to emphasize that the doing of social science is a dynamic and ongoing activity. The emphasis is on how science is done rather than on the products science produces. The social scientist ought not construct a theory and then, as he might with a static museum piece, stand back and inspect it indefinitely. Rather, he ought to look constantly for the neutral analogy portions of the model in order to make new predictions. The results of these tested predictions then can be used to elaborate or revise the theory which, in turn, produces slightly different portions of the neutral analogy which, in its turn, allows for different predictions to be made. The process of using the neutral analogy portions of the analogue, functioning as a model for the theory under investigation, continues in this fashion indefinitely.

The term *Pragmatics* was chosen for the title to emphasize that the use of analogues as models for theories is not mere scientific or intellectual window-dressing but is essential to the doing of social science. The systematic testing, elaborating, and modifying of theories rests on continually identifying the neutral analogy portions of the analogue used as the model for the theory. Without an appropriate analogue and its attendant portions of neutral analogy, the testing of theory would proceed on a more random, hit-or-miss basis—if at all.

In short, the social scientist must be able to see similarities between phenomena where others see only differences. In this respect he is like any creative person—humanist or otherwise. The scientist creates his instruments as does the humanist. And the theory or model which results from using the instrument is the scientist's creation just as is the poem resulting from the poet's application of his instruments.

The book does not dwell on the issue of similarities and differences between scientists and humanists. Having made an argument, I move on to discuss *what* the social scientist does to construct theories and models of social behavior, as well as *how* and *why* he engages in such activity. The book is intended to be neither a "cookbook" containing easy to follow recipes for concocting theories and models nor is it intended to be a treatise on the philosophy of social science. It aims at a blend of the two.

Developing theories and models that produce worthwhile questions cannot be taught completely by prescription. It is this rather simple fact that makes the doing of social science exciting. These is no statistic or design per se that can replace human imagination and insight. But statistics and designs can be used imaginatively to ask previously unaskable questions. It is our ability to think creatively, not our ability to follow prescribed procedures uncritically, that characterizes social science at its best. It is a more substantive understanding of what social science is that this book tries to provide.

The book is divided roughly into three sections. Chapters 1 and 2 provide the philosophic backdrop against which the remaining chapters are to be interpreted. Chapter 1 makes the assumption that the basic tool of the scientist is language; consequently that chapter is a discussion of the language of science. Chapter 2 addresses itself specifically to the scientific attitude; the frame of mind, if you will, in which science is accomplished.

The second section consists of Chapters 3 through 8 and focuses on "how" and "why" theories are constructed. Chapter 3 is a treatment of general issues of theory construction. Chapters 4 through 7 are detailed descriptions of four different types of theories. Chapter 8 concerns itself with the explanatory role and function of theories.

The last general section is concerned with scientific models, how they are built, and how they complement theories. Chapter 9 is the counterpart of Chapter 3; it takes up the basic issues involved in model building. Chapter 10 narrows in focus and discusses specific structures, substances, and types of models. Chapter 11 offers three examples of descriptive models of communication. Each model is explicated in some detail. Chapter 12 deals with three explicative models and one simulative model of communication.

Reading prefaces of books, I was always struck by what I thought was a mere formality; acknowledging wives, children, pets, typewriter repairmen, and colleagues (not necessarily listed in order of importance) for their assistance during the writing of the book. But after laboring over this manuscript I have lost much of that cynicism. During the writing I was so drawn into the ideas that I truly lost perspective of the entire effort at times.

Several of my colleagues at Ohio State read early versions of parts of the manuscript and pointed out weaknesses and blind spots. Robert Nofsinger, Thomas McCain, and David Smith were never convinced by all of the arguments I advanced and in disagreeing they strengthened the final product. David Mortensen at Wisconsin and Ronald Geizer at Minnesota reviewed the first draft of the complete manuscript and their critical evaluations resulted in several important changes in the final product.

I am particularly grateful to Peter Monge at San José for his careful reading of the manuscript and a page-by-page critique and suggestion list of changes and additions. Many of those changes Peter will recognize as having been incorporated into the final draft. On many points Peter and I are still in disagreement, but having pointed them out he gave me the opportunity to rethink my own position. Particularly, Peter was critical of basing a method of theory construction on the logic of analogy. I address that issue in Chapter One using Peter's own argument and respond with some material he suggested I consider. Opportunities for such intellectual debate are far too rare and I appreciate Peter's taking time to engage me in some of the issues related to the book.

To Robert L. Scott, for whom science devoid of metaphor can have no philosophical base; and to Karl Weick, a model and teacher of scientific analogue construction, this student owes a large debt.

In the process of writing I came to realize how important several people are whom I normally take for granted; my wife, a close colleague, a dear friend, my secretary, a hated enemy, and a discreet mistress. Laina may never know how much of her is in this book.

Finally, special thanks to the Department of Health, Education, and Welfare under whose sponsorship through grant #OEG-0-72-4520 portions of this manuscript were prepared.

*Columbus, Ohio*                                            **L.C.H.**
*February 1975*

# Contents

## 5   Type II Theory:
### Duncan's Theory of Social Order

## 6   Type III Theory:
### Ego-Involvement Theory

## 7   Type IV Theory:
### Information Theory

## 8   Theory as Explanation

*Perhaps every science must start with metaphor and end with algebra; and perhaps without the metaphor there would never have been any algebra.*

**MAX BLACK** *Models and Metaphors*

**1**

# The Language of Science

## INTRODUCTION

The social scientist's primary task is to explain all manner of human behavior. Such explanations are referred to as theories and models and to construct them the scientist needs a language. In some instances the language is verbal; in other instances it may be mathematical. But whatever the form used, language is the scientist's most fundamental instrument for without it he could not do science.

This chapter examines those dimensions of language most intimately related to the work of social scientists. If we are to understand why and how the social scientist does science, we must first understand the basic tools with which he works. One reason man is the only animal we know of who can do science is that man is the only animal we know of who can use signs as symbols in complex higher order patterns. It is man's ability to symbolize that enables him to conceptualize and exploit the metaphorical dimensions of language and explain his own behavior. It is with this understanding that our discussion of language and science begins.

## SYMBOLS AS CONCEPTS

The social sciences and the humanities have one important common denominator; the object of their respective studies is man, his thoughts and actions. Unlike the natural scientist, who is concerned with natural phenomena extrinsic to himself, the social scientist is himself a representative of the phenomena he investigates. Scholars interested in man—whether they be social scientists, novelists, literary critics, poets, or mystics—agree, either implicitly or explicitly, that man has a unique capability among all animals; man can symbolize.

All animals, including man, live in a world made up of signs; stimuli from the physical and nonphysical objects in the world. It is generally agreed that there are two types of signs which are defined by the ways animals respond to them—signals and symbols. With the exception of man, all animals are restricted to the use of signals. Signals are stimuli which have come to be associated with various physical objects. Pavlov's dog salivating at the sound of a bell is a good example of an animal responding to a signal. Over a period of experimental trials, a bell immediately precedes a presentation of food to the dog. The dog is hungry and salivates when he sees and smells the food. After a while the dog associates the bell signal with imminent presentation of food. In short, the bell has come to signal food for the dog. He will salivate when he hears the bell because the bell signals food.

## Conceptualizing

Man uses and relies on signals too, from bells on ovens, buzzers on clocks, and lights at intersections. But man has the capacity to use signs as symbols. Symbols are signs which lead to the *conceptualization* of their referents. The sign need not be present and the referent need not be a physical object. We cannot tell Pavlov's dog to imagine that a steak is in front of him, when in fact there is no steak present, and expect the dog to salivate. The dog cannot use signs to conceptualize a steak; he requires the sign to be present physically; that is, either the steak or the ringing bell must be present. But we can tell a hungry man to imagine a steak (assuming he knows what a steak is) and expect him to lick his lips or comment on how good it is going to taste. The man can use our description (signs) as symbols; he can conceptualize a steak.

In the above example, the referent of the sign was a physical object. But man also can use signs as symbols to conceptualize nonphysical or abstract referents. He can talk about attitudes, institutions, emotions, egos, etc., even though each of these words (signs used as symbols) has no physical referent that can be apprehended with our five senses. It is not surprising that we call such symbols *concepts;* signs are used as symbols which lead to the *conceptualization* or imagination of referents. Bronowski (1965) says of signs used as symbols or concepts, "the name or symbol remains present, and the mind works with it when the thing is absent" (p.32). For Pavlov's dog, or anyone else's dog for that matter, the bell is a signal but the word s-t-e-a-k is not used as a symbol or concept.

## LANGUAGE AS METAPHOR

Man's symbols are not randomly arranged signs which lead to the conceptualization of isolated and discrete referents. Rather, man's symbols are arranged in a systematic or patterned fashion with certain rules governing their usage. This arrangement of symbols is called a language and the rules which influence the patterning and usage of the symbols constitute the grammar of the language. To say that man uses symbols linguistically is to say that man can arrange symbols in various patterns which lead to the conceptualization of various referents and patterns of referents. Man can think abstractly and this attribute sets him apart from lower animal forms.

It is a very small step from saying man's language is symbolic to saying that man's language is metaphoric. Some (e.g., Black, 1962; and Campbell, 1972) have argued that all language is metaphor. Richards (1936) defines metaphor as "fundamentally a borrowing between and intercourse of *thoughts,* a transaction between contexts" (p.94). Later he says a metaphor is two ideas "which co-operate in an inclusive meaning" (p.119).

## Types of Metaphor

Black (1962) describes three different uses of the term *metaphor* and we will paraphrase his discussion to clarify how that term will be used throughout this book. The "substitution view of metaphor" considers a metaphorical expression to be the equivalent of a literal expression. From this perspective, metaphors are simply linguistic decorations because they communicate more ornately what could have been communicated in literal, straightforward language. This definition of metaphor assumes that not all language is metaphoric. It is possible to communicate using literal language, and metaphors are window dressing. They are interesting little linguistic puzzles that the reader can decode by finding the literal expression that can be substituted for the metaphoric expression (pp.32–34).

The "comparison view of metaphor" is really a special case of the "substitution view." The "comparison view" uses metaphors as substitutes for literal *comparisons* rather than literal *expressions.* The metaphor is thought to present an underlying analogy or similarity (pp.35–37). Black uses an example to make the distinction clear.

> The chief difference between a substitution view ... and the special form of it that I have called a comparison view may be illustrated by the stock example of "Richard is a lion." On the first view, the sentence means approximately the same as "Richard is brave;" on the second, approximately the same as "Richard is *like* a lion [in being brave]," the added words in

brackets being understood but not explicitly stated. In the second translation, as in the first, the metaphorical statement is taken to be standing in place of some literal equivalent. But the comparison view provides a more elaborate paraphrase, inasmuch as the original statement is interpreted as being about lions as well as about Richard (p.36).

But in many instances the metaphor *creates* the similarity rather than presents an already existing similarity. Black says metaphors that create similarities where none existed conform to the "interaction view of metaphor." This view is much like Richards's (1936) definition of metaphor. Two ideas, symbols, or concepts previously thought to be unrelated are combined and certain similarities are created resulting in a new idea, symbol, or concept. Again, Black provides an example.

We may discover what is here intended by applying Richards' remark to our earlier example, "The poor are the Negroes of Europe." The substitution view, at its crudest, tells us that something is being said indirectly about the poor of Europe. (But what? That they are an oppressed class, a standing reproach to the community's ideals, that poverty is inherited and indelible?) The comparison view claims that the epigram presents some comparison between the poor and the Negroes. In opposition to both, Richards says that our "thoughts" about European poor and American Negroes are "active together" and "interact" to produce a meaning that is a resultant of that interaction (p.38).

Throughout this book, when the term *metaphor* is used it refers to the "interaction" point of view. As will be demonstrated in subsequent chapters, metaphors are basic to the doing of science not because of their figurative or substitution value but because they create new concepts and organize our thinking.

## Characteristics of Metaphors

To crystalize the "interaction view of metaphor" and to provide a specific reference for further discussion, Black's seven characteristics of this view are presented.

1.   A metaphorical statement has two distinct subjects—a "principal" subject and a "subsidiary" one.

2.   These subjects are often best regarded as "systems of things," rather than "things."

3.   The metaphor works by applying to the principal subject a system of "associated implications" characteristic of the subsidiary subject.

4.   These implications usually consist of "commonplaces" about the subsidiary subject, but may, in suitable cases, consist of deviant implications established *ad hoc* by the writer.

5.   The metaphor selects, emphasizes, suppresses, and organizes features of the principal subject by implying statements about it that normally apply to the subsidiary subject.

6.   This involves shifts in meaning of words belonging to the same family or system as the metaphorical expression; and some of these shifts, though not all, may be metaphorical transfers. (The subordinate metaphors are, however, to be read less "emphatically.")

7.   There is, in general, no simple "ground" for the necessary shifts of meaning—no blanket reason why some metaphors work and others fail (pp.44–45).

Notice the similarity between symbol and metaphor. A symbol involves three elements; a sign, a referent to which it is applied, and the concept which is *re-presented.* A metaphor also involves three elements; a principal subject, a subsidiary subject, and the shift in meaning resulting from their combination. Symbols and metaphors are both products of abstract, creative processes.

By virtue of being symbolic in nature, man's language is metaphoric. This is to say neither that man consciously creates metaphors when he uses language nor that all metaphors are equally provocative in their resultant conceptualizations. For example, Raser (1969) quotes Fowler as saying, "Strictly speaking, metaphor occurs as often as we take a word out of its original sphere and apply it to new circumstances" (p.5). Fowler points out that there are eight different metaphors in that sentence. But there is nothing very useful in digging out the eight metaphors in his sentence. The example simply points out that language is constituted of symbols and that symbols and metaphors are implicit or explicit creations of similarities between concepts. The doing of science rests on the exploitation of provocative metaphors because such metaphors suggest specific analogies that produce questions the answers to which serve as explanations of human behavior.

## Analogies

An analogy, as defined in the American Heritage Dictionary, is a "correspondence in some respects, especially in function or position, between things otherwise dissimilar." Analogies, then, are the embodiment of implicit questions, primarily questions of structure and function. For example, what are the structural and functional similarities between man's information processing behavior and the information processing behavior of a computer? In what ways is the relationship between a husband and wife similar to the relationship between two negotiating attorneys? What are the similarities between economic exchange resulting in debits and credits and social interaction? These are the types of questions implicit in using a computer as an analogue for man's brain, a partial conflict relationship as an analogue for a marital relationship, and economics as an analogue for social interaction.

In a sense, metaphors *express* or *suggest* analogies that can be constructed in some detail. The structural and functional properties of the "principal" subject or analogue are applied to and combined with the structural and functional properties of the "subsidiary" subject. The questions generated are usually questions regarding the applicability of the combination of subjects or concepts.

## Faults of Analogies

There is a danger in relying on analogues too heavily or too uncritically as a basis for the construction of theories and models. The same criticisms as are applied to reasoning from analogy in argumentation are pertinent here. Buck (1956) contends that analogies could be drawn between virtually any dimensions of phenomena and that for every analogy many disanalogies could also be made. In a more recent critique of the explanatory value of analogy, Bunge (1970) concludes:

> Likewise, arguments from analogy, although individually analyzable, do not seem amenable to theoretical systematization,

and this for two reasons. First, because they are all invalid; second, because their fruitfulness depends on the nature of the case. In short, no logic of analogy seems to be possible (p.34).

I am not taking the position that analogies may be used uncritically as the basis for constructing theories and models. Nor am I suggesting that a logic of analogy is possible. I am saying that analogies are used *primarily* during the inductive or "discovery" phase of scientific inquiry. I emphasize the qualifier "primarily" because I am in agreement with the position George de Santillana (1941) articulated writing on "Aspects of Scientific Rationalism in the Nineteenth Century." "There is never a 'strict induction' but contains a considerable amount of deduction, starting from points chosen analogically" (p.7).

Richard Weaver (1953), in his essay on "The Rhetoric of Social Science," continues on this same point.

> In other words, analogy formulates and to some extent directs the inquiry. Any investigation must start from certain minimal likenesses, and that may conceal the truth that some analogy lies at the heart of all assertion. Even Bertrand Russell is compelled to accept analogy as one of the postulates required to validate the scientific method because it provides the antecedent probability necessary to justify an induction. . . .
>
> Our naive question, "What is it like?" which we ask of anything we are confronting for the first time is the intellect's cry for help. Unless it is like something in some measure, we shall never get to understand it (p.204).

Analogues are the basis for all theories and models and their heuristic utility is determined empirically over time as questions which the analogues generate are answered. The work of the social scientist just begins when an analogue is used to develop a theory or model; the explanatory usefulness of that analogue must be assessed empirically.

## STYLES OF THINKING

We have been alluding to similarities and differences in styles of thought that characterize the scientist and the artist. Before going

further it is necessary to define several different styles of symbolizing or thinking. Kaplan (1964) differentiates six styles of thought in
the social sciences (pp.259–262). His classification is based on the
extent to which each style relies on the language of mathematics.
Although Kaplan classifies styles of thinking in the social sciences
—which does not include poetic styles, for example—it is safe to
assume that such styles would make even less use of the language
of mathematics than do those six he does treat.

It should be made clear at the outset that one style of thinking
is not inherently more or less preferable to another. Each is appropriate to types of questions being asked and what counts as an
answer. If one is interested in the *unique* attributes of a particular
historical or contemporary figure or social condition, an answer
couched in the language of mathematics probably would be unsatisfactory. On the other hand, if one is seeking a *general* explanation
of bargaining behavior, analyzing individual bargaining cases would
be an inefficient course to pursue. It should be noted, however, that
as scientific disciplines mature, their questions and explanations
become more encompassing, general, and therefore more amenable to being stated in the most general of all languages—mathematics.

## Literary

The first style of thinking, and the least mathematical, Kaplan
(1964) calls *literary*. "This cognitive style is likely to be occupied
with individuals, particular persons or sets of events, case studies,
clinical findings, and the like. . . . A person, a movement, or a whole
culture is interpreted, but largely in terms of the specific purposes
and perspectives of the actors, rather than in terms of the abstract
and general categories of the scientist's own explanatory scheme"
(p.259).

It is not being concerned with the purposes and perspectives
of the actors but rather the level of abstractness of the language
used that renders the literary style unscientific. The concern of
someone relying on a literary style is usually the description of
persons and events as relatively unique phenomena. Much of literary and rhetorical criticism (e.g., Thonssen and Baird, 1948; Black,
1965; and Burke, 1941, 1945, c1950, 1953, 1954) as well as some
literatures of anthropology (e.g., Malinowski, 1948; Levi-Strauss,
1969; and Radcliffe-Brown, 1924, 1949), psychiatry (e.g., Freud,

1949, 1953; Jung, 1950; and Adler, 1935), and clinical sociology (e.g., Dumont, 1969; Feinberg, 1968; and Grier and Cobbs, 1968) are cast in the literary style. The concern is with a detailed critical treatment of a rhetorical, literary, or somehow different individual or group of individuals. The emphasis is on characteristic differences rather than on general statements of differences and similarities.

## Academic

The second style of thought Kaplan calls *academic.* "There is some attempt to be precise, but it is verbal rather than operational. . . . The materials dealt with tend to be ideational rather than observational data, and their treatment tends to be highly theoretical, if not, indeed, purely speculative" (p.259).

Particular schools of thought or individual thinkers can be identified by characteristic idioms and recurrent metaphors used to explain the subject matter. In sociology, for example, the writings of Tarde (1969), Parsons (1937), Durkheim (1933), and more recently Duncan (1962, 1968) are in the academic style. Each is identifiable by the recurrent metaphors exploited and idioms used to achieve verbal clarity. Parsons builds most of his speculative theory on a mechanistic metaphor whereas Duncan's speculative theory rests on a dramatistic metaphor that draws heavily from Burke. Burke's literary criticism, in turn, is grounded in a literary-religious metaphor. None of these works is supported by observational data although they do make an effort to be precise at a verbal level. This is the primary reason why the writing style of *academic* thinkers is characteristic; each uses language in a characteristic way in attempting to be precise.

## Eristic

Kaplan's third cognitive style is *eristic.* "Here there is a strong interest in proof, and of specific propositions, rather than, as in the literary and academic styles, the aim only of exhibiting the cognitive possibilities in certain broad perspectives on the subject matter. Experimental and statistical data become important. Attention is given to deductive relationships, logical derivations from propositions previously established or explicitly assumed, though proofs are sketched rather than rigorously laid out" (p.260). This style of thinking and writing is most predominant in the social sciences today. Most of the social science journals contain at least some articles representing this eristic method of operation. The heavy reliance on statistics to model the data obtained and the interest in testing for statistically significant differences is characteristic.

Speech communication, social psychology, and sociology are the social sciences most actively engaged in generating knowledge via the eristic style. Perhaps the most active research areas are persuasion or attitude change (see e.g., Cohen, 1964; Fishbein, 1967, 1973; Insko, 1967; Abelson *et al.*, 1968; and Miller, 1973) and small group behavior (see e.g., Bales, 1950, 1972; Maier, 1963; McGrath and Altman, 1966; Dunphy, 1972; and Lieberman *et al.*, 1973). The typical research strategy is to identify a concept of interest—whether it be type of persuasive argument, credibility of the speaker, involvement of the listener, style of group leadership, number of persons in the group, or whatever—and then determine how changing that concept in some way influences other important concepts. Statistics are used to determine whether the changes that result are significant in a statistical sense. Special theories and models of this line of inquiry will be treated in detail in subsequent chapters.

## Symbolic

This style of thinking, which is Kaplan's fourth, may be confusing because of his use of the word "symbolic" and the way that term was used earlier in this chapter. However, Kaplan uses the term in a specific way whereas we were using it in its generic form. Kaplan says, "In the symbolic style, mathematics comes into its own. It is not, however, the rigor of mathematical demonstration which is significant, but the precision and power of mathematic ideas. The subject matter is conceptualized from the outset in mathematical terms. Both problems and solutions are formulated, therefore, in a more or less artificial language; neologisms abound, and special notations are introduced for the purposes required by the context. . . . Statistical data do not serve, as in the eristic style, only as a body of evidence; they are processed so as to generate new hypotheses, and even new patterns of conceptualization" (p.260).

In subsequent chapters we will be examining several theories and models cast in the symbolic style. For the moment, however, it is sufficient to point out that mathematical forms such as regression and differential equations are used to display relationships among concepts which may or may not have been surfaced in eristically oriented research (Lazarsfeld, 1969; and Kemeny and Snell, 1962). For example, suppose we found that in a discussion group the extent to which people talked to each other was determined by status in the group, the amount of time each spends talking, people's power over one another, and the proximity of the group members (Collins and Guetzkow, 1964, p.187). This finding could be stated in the symbolic style in the form of a set of regression equations (Monge, 1973, p.15). The reason for choosing the symbolic style of expression is because statements can be subjected to mathematically standardized transformations as a way of systematically deriving new questions; questions which may not have been noticed if the relationships among the concepts had been left in an academic or eristic style. In a sense, mathematical transformations allow us to be insightful in more rigorous and systematic ways.

## Postulational

Of this style Kaplan says, "This has many of the characteristics of the symbolic style, of which, indeed, it could be regarded as a special variant. It differs from the symbolic style in general only as logic differs from mathematics. The validity of proof is at the focus of attention here, rather than the content of the propositions which occur at the various steps" (p.261).

Information theory is a good example of a theory cast in the postulational style (Shannon and Weaver, 1964). In simplified terms, Shannon and Weaver were concerned with the most efficient way of coding and sending more than one message at the same time over the same channel. They wanted the most efficient code for the messages so that many could be sent without being distorted by noise or static. They began by laying out a series of statements that were taken on their face value to be true. These statements are called postulates (hence the term *postulational* style). From these postulational statements other statements—called theorems—are derived. The emphasis of a theory cast in postulational style is not so much to verify and explain "substance" or empirical content but rather to validate the "form" or logical accuracy of the given set of postulates which serve as initial assumptions. Thus a theory cast in postulational style generates *formal knowledge* deductively. Knowledge is expanded in a conditional fashion; *if* the postulates are true, *then* the theorems deduced from those postulates are true. This form of proof is said to be logically circular or *tautological* inasmuch as the theorems serve as logical proof of the postulates, which is where the theorems came from in the first place.

The objective of a postulational explanation is the simplest set of postulates that will generate theorems which account for any phenomenon having similar form. In this sense a postulational theory is not a substantive theory but a formal theory; its objective is not to explain some particular content but to derive a logical structure that may be the form of several other subject matters. Kaplan says that a good postulational theory is one which allows for elegant proofs of the important propositions of the subject matter. He stresses, indirectly, the importance of an aesthetically constructed theory. Shannon and Weaver's information theory is widely respected as a postulational theory because a relatively few number of postulates produce a wide range of theorems.

## Formal

The last style Kaplan describes is the *formal* style.

> This is very close to the postulational style, and indeed, presupposes the latter. The difference is that here the key terms are not given any interpretation; there is no reference to any specific empirical content. What is remarkable is that the validity of the derivations is not dependent upon any such content, but only upon the pattern of relationships holding among the symbols themselves—hence the designation 'formal'. . . . Because of the multiplicity of interpretations which it allows, a formal system has the immediate advantage of possible application to a variety of subject matters, which are thereby shown to have the same formal structure (p.262).

Geometry, algebra, and calculus are examples of formal languages.

If we differentiate among the six styles of thinking according to form and content, explanations cast in the literary style are primarily content-oriented and minimally concerned with the underlying structure or form of that content. Explanations in the formal style, on the other hand, are minimally interested in specific content and maximally concerned with abstract forms or structures. The more content-oriented the explanation, the more it must rely on verbal and statistical language. The more form-oriented the explanation, the more it must rely on mathematical and logical language.

Your style of thinking or symbolizing influences the metaphors with which you become familiar. This, in turn, influences the analogies made apparent and therefore the questions you ask. The nature of the questions influences the answers or explanations you consider satisfactory. If you think in a literary style, you are more likely to ask questions growing out of literary analogies and, therefore, verbal answers are counted as explanations. On the other hand, if you think in a formal style, you are more likely to ask questions which grow out of logical analogies and, therefore, mathematical answers are counted as explanations.

Not all of the social sciences are sufficiently developed, in terms of empirical data and eristic theories, to ask formal questions and expect formal answers. This is not to say that such disciplines are not amenable to formal analyses. It is to say that sufficient information must be available before formal structures of data can be ascertained. Typically, inquiry conducted in literary and academic styles is not considered to be scientific. To understand why this is the case, the attitude of scientific inquiry must be made clear.

*As attending to art begins with "the willing suspension of disbelief," social science starts with a willed suspension of belief. In the ordinary business of living we are accustomed to accept on faith a fantastically complex set of assumptions about the social world and the actors in it; this is what is meant by "culture." The social scientist, reversing Hamlet, always suspects that "there are more things in your philosophy than Heaven and Earth have dreamed of."*

**SCOTT GREER**   *The Logic of Social Inquiry*

**2**

# The Scientific Attitude

## INTRODUCTION

The remainder of this book demonstrates how symbols and metaphors—the language of science—are used to shape theories and models of human behavior. The process which begins with metaphor and ends with model is the doing of science. But to have a clear understanding of this process it is essential to distinguish between what science *is* and what it *is not*. Before discussing the scientific attitude in specifics, some conceptions of science which are attributed wrongfully to that activity are examined.

## MISCONCEPTIONS OF SCIENCE

The poet, novelist, mystic, theologian, and scientist are all human beings and therefore symbol users and members of a language community. Each relies on and exploits the metaphoric nature of language to create his respective explanation of human phenomena. The explanations differ insofar as the analogies produced are combinations of different concepts. They also differ in terms of what is done to and with the analogy once formulated. But the undeniable fact is that poetry, novels, myths, dogmas, theories, and models are all symbolic creations of man.

Bronowski (1965) argues that the symbol and the metaphor are as necessary to science as they are to poetry inasmuch as all science, like all art, is the search for unity in hidden likeness (pp.13, 36). Too frequently this fundamental similarity between the arts, humanities, and sciences either is overlooked or misunderstood. The shortsighted artist, humanist, and scientist look at one another and see a division between them where none exists. The irony is that they do not understand very clearly their own domains. The shortsighted scientist is frequently as unclear about the nature of science as he is about the nature of art. The same is true of the shortsighted artist and humanist. Each unwittingly is vulnerable to the criticisms of the other. The results are unfortunate misconceptions.

### Subjective vs Objective

Perhaps the most pervasive misconception is that the arts and humanities are subjective and intuitive whereas science is objective and methodical. As in most misconceptions, there is a grain of truth in this one. The error is in the exaggeration. The scientist often is viewed as a person who spends his professional life objectively and unemotionally cataloguing "facts" which he obtains by using certain accepted procedures to observe, in an unbiased way, naturally occurring events. His goal is thought to be a detailed re-presentation of the "reality" that exists "out there." The scientist supposedly "discovers" nature's hidden secrets; the secrets are thought to exist *a priori* and it is the job of the scientist to use his objective tools to make wondrous "discoveries."

The artist or humanist, on the other hand, frequently is viewed as a creative, intuitive person who relies on his subjective experiences as sources of insight. Unlike the scientist, the artist is quite emotional and temperamental. He wants to "touch and feel" all of life whereas the scientist wants to stand back and objectively observe. Supposedly, the artist is not concerned with a "reality" that "really exists out there" but with his subjective and internal reactions to it. The artist is thought not to be concerned with "truth" but rather with aesthetically pleasing renderings of "universal human feelings."

## Aesthetics vs Pragmatics

A misconception much along these same lines is that science is pragmatic because it results in useful products whereas art is a more aesthetic undertaking and results in products which affect our senses but which have little, if any, practical application. After all, goes the misconception, science has given us all manner of handy gadgets, technological breakthroughs like computers, and has even put men on the moon. What has art ever done to rival these accomplishments?

## The Creative Act

The common element of "original" science and art, however, is the creative intellectual act. "The discoveries of science, the works of art are explorations—more, are explosions of a hidden likeness. The discoverer or the artist presents in them two aspects of nature and fuses them into one. This is the act of creation, in which an original thought is born, and it is the same act in original science and original art" (Bronowski, 1965, p.19). The scientist is not a camera or computer. He cannot, even if he wanted to, passively and unemotionally observe and catalogue. Like the artist, he creates a conceptualization of the world around him. A catalogue of observed events is no more a science than a pile of bricks is a building. It is not the "facts" that characterize science but rather the ingenious combining of those facts into the scientist's creation—the model and theory.

From such a perspective, science is not the re-presenting of an "objective reality out there" but is rather a systematic mining of metaphors and analogies which suggest explanations of phenomena that are accepted for a time. Granted the theories and models, as scientific creations, must meet certain pragmatic criteria to survive for any length of time. But theories and models, as will be seen later, also must meet certain aesthetic criteria; they should be elegant in terms of symmetry and parsimony.

## Science and Aesthetics

The artist, on the other hand, does not have unlimited freedom to indulge his idiosyncratic fantasies. There are certain artistic and aesthetic standards which are used to assess the various artistic media and their products. These standards can be and are applied to the works of art to determine their contribution to the world of art (Aldrich, 1963). Granted, there are disagreements over the merits of certain art forms. But there are equally heated disagreements over the merits of given lines of scientific inquiry. The difference between art and science, then, cannot be the fact that science is objective and methodical and art is subjective and intuitive. Both involve the use of symbols, both are creative, both rely on metaphors and analogies, and the merits of both are difficult to determine. Both the artist and the scientist are human beings using symbols to create explanations or accounts of human activity.

Perhaps the one characteristic of science most frequently overlooked is that it has an aesthetic dimension. Bronowski (1965) concludes his chapter on the creative mind by saying, "Science, like art, is not a copy of nature but a re-creation of her. We re-make nature by the act of discovery, in the poem or in the theorem. And the great poem and the deep theorem are new to every reader, and yet are his own experiences, because he himself re-creates them. They are the marks of unity in variety; and in the instant when the mind seizes this for itself, in art or in science, the heart misses a beat" (p.20).

## Origins and Destinations

The foregoing discussion was not to say that art and science are synonymous activities. Art and science do differ markedly from one another, but the difference is in the destination rather than the origin of their respective efforts. The origin of both is the creative act of insight made possible by the use of symbols. Both are attempting to create and re-create order out of chaos, likeness out of unlikeness. The artist frames his analogy and its parent metaphor so that the insightful reader can tease out interpretations and implications. This is true also of the scientist. Both the work of art and the scientific theory or model derive their aesthetic qualities from their respective forms. But the artist is not concerned that all observers or readers arrive at their interpretations of his work via the steps of logic; the scientist is. To put the matter another way, the scientist is concerned with the *logical* verification of his work whereas the artist is concerned primarily with *psychological* verification.

Once the work of art is completed, the art community assesses it, but not with the objective of changing it if it does not conform to already existing works. But the work of science, if logical verification so demonstrates, must be changed to conform to the existing body of knowledge. Bronowski (1965) claims, "The creative act is alike in art and in science; but it cannot be identical in the two; there must be a difference as well as a likeness. For example, the artist in his creation surely has open to him a dimension of freedom which is closed to the scientist. I have insisted that the scientist does not merely record the facts; but he must conform to the facts. The sanction of truth is an exact boundary which encloses him, in a way in which it does not constrain the poet or the painter" (p.28).

In a sense, the artist exploits the psychological dimensions of ambiguity whereas the scientist works to logically minimize that ambiguity. Not only does the scientist try to minimize the ambiguity of his metaphors and analogies but the analogues, and the facts they account for or explain, must conform to other facts which the scientific community, at that point in time, considers to be the best explanation. This same criterion does not bind the artist. His work must conform to the currently held standards of aesthetics. But there is no additional "objective truth criterion" to which the artist's work is subjected.

## PHASES OF SCIENTIFIC INQUIRY

The doing of science is basically a puzzle or problem-solving activity (Kuhn, 1962). Some problem becomes apparent and the scientist attempts to solve it. For example, the problem may be phrased as a question, "how is man's ability to process information similar to a computer's ability to process information?" This question emerges from an analogy that takes instances of two different categories (the computer is an instance of the category "machine" and man is an instance of the category "animal") and combines them into a third and different category ("behavior") to determine similarities in function. Recall that an analogy is defined as an instance of two dissimilar elements being compared in terms of structure and/or function. The problem to be solved is how well the two dissimilar elements fit together in chosen respects.

### Inducing

Kemeny and Snell (1962) identify three phases of scientific inquiry. First is the step of *induction* which carries the scientist from factual observation to the formation of theories. Kemeny and Snell acknowledge that the inductive step is necessarily creative even though rules have been proposed for systematizing observation procedures. As Bronowski (1965) stated earlier, order is not discovered but is created out of disorder. The world as it exists "out there" is, to borrow William James's phrase, a "booming, buzzing confusion." If a scientist's job were merely to observe and record his observations, the results would be a jumbled, senseless catalogue of all manner of activity. So during the inductive phase, the scientist is confronted with two problems; what to observe and once having observed it, how the observations should be "put together" into an orderly account of (or theory of) what was observed. A theory, as we shall see later, is more than a sequence of observations. It is a unique ordering or patterning of observations in a way that explains something not observed directly.

A person adept at observing and recording what he sees around him but with no apparent reason for or strategy of selecting certain phenomena to observe is not a scientist. The reason to observe in the first place is to acquire information that will help solve the apparent problem.

The scientist, however, cannot observe all instances of the problem he is trying to solve. If he is trying to answer, for example, how rumors spread in a community, he cannot observe every instance of rumors being spread in all communities. He must be satisfied with making a limited number of observations of the rumor phenomenon and then attempt to generalize from those limited observations. In this sense, even an inspired and creative theory is, in part, an inspired guess; a guess that what was observed in a limited number of instances would have been observed in all instances if all the instances had been observed.

## Deducing

Because the inductive phase requires educated guesswork, it is important to determine how accurate or satisfactory the educated guess (theory) is of how rumors are transmitted. Kemeny and Snell (1962) indicate that it is at this stage of inquiry that the tools of logic and mathematics come into play. The second phase of scientific inquiry is *deduction* which is the derivation of consequences from the proposed theory. Many of these consequences may not have been apparent to the scientist without the application of the formal tools of mathematics and logic. In many instances of social science theory construction, however, the consequences derived from theory are based on common sense and speculation rather than on rigorous deductive analysis. But either in logical deduction or common sense speculation, the purpose is to complete the theory in more detail and, at the same time, to specify the conditions that should hold true if the theory is viable.

## Verifying

The third phase of scientific inquiry is *verification*. This is the stage in which the derivation of the theory is tested to determine if it holds true. In the social sciences, experimentation is the usual procedure for verifying a theory. If the verifications support the consequences, the theory is said to be supported. If the verifications do not support the consequences, the scientist is in a quandary. One explanation is that the theory is deficient and therefore the derived consequence of the theory is faulty. On the other hand, the scientist may have done a poor job setting up his test of those consequences. Thus answers to problems provide new problems to be solved. A theory is constantly in a state of being supported or being modified.

It is in the process of verifying theories that prediction plays a central role. The consequences of a theory are statements phrased in conditional form. For example, if the spreading of rumors is like the spreading of a disease, then. . . . If the antecedent condition is correct, then the consequent condition should result. An experiment is a way of testing the statement by predicting what should happen under certain antecedent conditions. Handy (1964) says, in his essay on the methodology of the social sciences, that "what is here understood by 'scientific inquiry' is the prediction and control (and/or adjustive behavior thereto) of events through the development of publicly verifiable warranted assertions that are subject to continuous criticism" (p.20).

## THE SCIENTIFIC ATTITUDE

The title of this section uses the term scientific *attitude* rather than the more common term *method* for several reasons. Method implies a set of rules, guidelines, or procedures to follow. Scientific inquiry generally does not follow the steps we just discussed. But doing science is not like baking a cake; it is more than a mechanical following of procedural steps. It is more than a method or series of methods. It presumes a certain frame of mind, perspective, or *attitude.* Method connotes procedures for answering questions whereas attitude connotes a perspective for asking questions.

In *The Sociological Imagination,* C. Wright Mills (1959) speaks directly to the issue of "the scientific method" by referring to several eminent scientists.

> Polykarp Kusch, Nobel Prize-winning physicist, has declared that there is no 'scientific method,' and that what is called by that name can be outlined for only quite simple problems. Percy Bridgman, another Nobel Prize-winning physicist, goes even further: 'There is no scientific method as such, but the vital feature of the scientist's procedure has been merely to do his utmost with his mind, *no holds barred.*' 'The mechanics of discovery,' William S. Beck remarks, 'are not known . . . I think that the creative process is so closely tied in with the emotional

structure of an individual . . . that . . . it is a poor subject for generalization. . . .' (p.58).

Polanyi (1946, 1959) and Bronowski (1965) make persuasive arguments for the contention that for science to exist at all, much less grow and prosper, there must be freedom to ask questions. Kuhn (1970), in his discussion of scientific revolutions, argues that existing paradigms are found to be inadequate when they no longer answer new questions being posed by scientists. The scientific attitude refers to an ever-present curiosity on the one hand and an ever-present suspicion on the other. The curiosity is manifested in the asking of questions and the suspicion is manifested in the uneasiness with existing answers. This uneasiness generates new questions. In the process of asking new questions and questioning old answers, there is no one method or procedure to follow. There is an array of approaches which is, in part, influenced by the scientist's style of thinking. But even within particular approaches, there is no consensus regarding what constitutes an appropriate question or an appropriate method for attempting an answer to the question.

## Method vs Attitude

Within the social science community, method frequently is mistaken for the conduct of scientific inquiry. To a certain extent, this is understandable although to understand it is not to condone it. Given that the social sciences want to become full-fledged members of the larger scientific community, it is not surprising that they would look to the more established sciences as models to emulate. For example, psychology primarily looked to physics and economics looked to applied mathematics. This has resulted in psychology's adoption of an eristic style of thought which produces impressive amounts of statistical data resulting from experimentation. In the case of economics, symbolic, postulational, and formal styles of thinking have produced mathematical models for a wide variety of economic phenomena. Speech communication is looking to the more established social sciences for models to emulate. To date, the one chosen almost exclusively has been social psychology and the method of experimentation.

There is nothing "bad" about one discipline adopting the methods of another. In fact, as we shall be discussing in subsequent chapters, such behavior is essential to the growth of knowledge. The danger is in assuming one particular style of thought and method to be the *only* scientific method. If this assumption is made, then anyone not using *the* method is thought to be unscientific. The harm of arbitrarily identifying a particular method or approach as scientific and excluding others is that needless time is wasted quibbling over the merits of different pieces of work, potentially valuable data are ignored, and most importantly, a misconception of science is perpetuated.

There is nothing inherently more scientific about mathematical methods than experimental methods, or experimental methods than field methods, or field methods than clinical methods. Each method is appropriate for a different style of thought and different levels of theoretical development. What is essential to scientific inquiry is that questions be asked so that procedures for answering the questions can be specified.

## "Scientific Truth"

Recall that science, unlike art and the humanities, is confronted with the sanction of truth. Inasmuch as truth does not exist "out there" in some a priori condition waiting for ingenious scientists to "discover" her, but rather is created by scientists out of an array of disordered phenomena, truth is whatever most of the scientists in a given area agree to be true at any given time. If any particular conception of truth is to achieve at least temporary consensus, the procedures that produce the information must be made public. Kaplan (1964) says truth should be thought of as the result of scientific inquiry properly conducted. If subsequent investigations produce information that corroborates previously obtained information, that particular conception of truth is further supported. If similar procedures yield dissimilar answers, the prevailing truth is cast in doubt. If differing answers are produced consistently following the same procedures, a new conception of truth must be created and temporarily accepted to account for the new answers.

## Operationalizing

The clearer the procedures are made for answering questions, the easier it will be to identify unsatisfactory questions and replace them with more appropriate ones. It is at this point that methods play a critical role in scientific inquiry. If concepts and procedures of testing or measuring the influence of concepts are not specified clearly, there is no way for other scientists to question the veracity of the answers produced. By not defining clearly the methods used, the scientific attitude is violated by making it impossible for others to check and build upon that work.

Insisting that concepts and procedures be defined and specified is not to say that some methods are better inherently than others. I can specify an experimental design and an appropriate statistic as clearly as I can specify a participant observation technique and an appropriate statistic. The difficulty confronting the social scientist is to ask appropriate questions and to select appropriate methods for answering them. Too frequently social scientists have what Kaplan (1964) calls a "trained incapacity" in this respect (p.28). He refers to this incapacity as "the law of the instrument" (pp.28–29). As a student, the social scientist becomes proficient in a particular method—whether it be factor analysis, analysis of variance, participant observation, criticism, or whatever—and subsequently asks only those questions to which he thinks his particular method will provide answers. Given the complexity of different methods and the need to specialize, this practice is understandable and, to some extent, necessary. But frequently the social scientist's trained incapacity leads him to believe that only those questions to which his method applies are worth asking.

Given that the scientific attitude is one of curiosity and suspicion, the scientist constantly is turning up new phenomena to explain and, at the same time, is questioning answers to previously studied phenomena. He does not assume that if he looks hard enough and long enough he will find truth once and for all. Rather he realizes that any conception of truth is imperfect. His quest is to propose conceptions of truth (theories) and then to evaluate them with the aim of deposing inadequate explanations in favor of more complete and internally consistent explanations (theories). In this respect, the scientific attitude encourages ongoing work; an ongoing search for questions which produce answers leading to more complete and consistent theories.

*The difference between a theoretical and descriptive formulation is like that between a metaphorical and literal statement.*

**ABRAHAM KAPLAN**   *The Conduct of Inquiry*

**3**

# Constructing Theory

## INTRODUCTION

Having considered the language and attitude of doing science, this chapter discusses their active use in the production of theory. More specifically, the different statements that can be used and the different arrangements of them are treated. It is demonstrated how different types of theory result from arranging the statements in various patterns. Examples from ego-involvement theory are used to clarify the discussion.

## THEORY AS METAPHOR

In Chapter 2 science was defined as a problem-solving activity. The problems of the social sciences are to explain presently unexplainable forms of human activity. Theories are constructed as temporary solutions or explanations. Kaplan (1964) puts it very simply; "A theory is a way of making sense of a disturbing situation. ..." (p.295). Because of man's ability to use symbols, however, he can learn *from* experience not just *by* it (Kaplan, 1964, p.295). Man can think about an event after it has occurred; he can think about parts of the event in the absence of that event.

Man's attempts to "make sense of disturbing situations" involve more than *describing* the situation, although description is a necessary first step. A description is *factual* insofar as it consists of concepts and observed instances of those concepts. For example, we might observe two people in a discussion group engaging in verbal conflict. A description of that situation would consist of listing different types (concepts) of verbal conflict and then sorting the observed behaviors into those types. The result is a series of *instances of concepts* (i.e., facts) but not an explanation of the situation.

### Relationship among Statements

A theory is designed to *explain how and why* the conflict occurred not just to describe *what* occurred. For a scientist to explain the facts of group conflict, he must put the facts into some order or pattern. He might list all the relevant facts of which he is aware. These facts are listed as declarative statements. His problem, like someone with all the jigsaw puzzle pieces before him, is how to "put the facts together." Unlike the jigsaw puzzle-solver, however, the facts do not have definite shapes; there is no one right way to assemble the facts. What gives a theory its power to explain is not the declarative statements it consists of but rather the relationship among those statements. It is the form of the relationship among statements rather than the individual statements themselves that distinguishes between theory and description.

The relationship among statements is the creation of the scientist. There is nothing about a fact, as there is about a jigsaw puzzle piece, that predetermines its relation to other pieces. In this respect, a theory is conjectural even though any one of its statements may be factual. A theory is metaphoric because "it reaches out beyond itself" and gropes for its denotation" (Kaplan, 1964, p.296). Creating relationships among statements is a symbolic activity; it is both an abstract and a conceptual process. Whereas facts are *perceived*, theories are *conceived*.

## THEORETICAL STATEMENTS

The building blocks of theory are descriptions of controlled observations. The observations are recorded as declarative statements consisting of two types of terms; *descriptive* and *logical*.

### Descriptive Terms

Descriptive terms are names for signs or attributes of signs. Such descriptive terms are called *concepts*. These concepts may be physical signs, which the five senses can apprehend directly; e.g., clouds, dogs, automobiles, and houses, or they may be abstract signs, which must be apprehended indirectly; e.g., attitude, value, ego, threat, and intelligence. In the latter instance, when signs are abstract and their attributes are not observable directly, concepts must be defined in such a way that they are scientifically useful. The usual procedure for doing so is to stipulate operations to be followed to make the abstract concept concrete.

This procedure is referred to as defining a concept operationally. For example, if a scientist wants to make a statement about the intelligence of a group of people, he must define intelligence so that other scientists will know exactly how he obtained his answer. The scientist may administer the Stanford-Binet intelligence test to all members of the group. A person's score on that test, then, is the operational definition of his intelligence. The other alternative would be to agree on what intelligence "really" is. But for the scientist, intelligence, like other concepts, does not "really" exist at all but is hypothetical; it is a scientific creation. Consequently, an "operation" like the Stanford-Binet test is agreed to be a useful index of an abstraction scientists call "intelligence." It is through this procedure of concretizing abstractions that we can talk of facts as instances of concepts *properly defined.*

Concepts are said to be *useful* when they are properly defined; they are said to be *meaningful* when they are systematically related to other concepts. "Intelligence," for example, becomes meaningful only when we understand its logical relationship to other concepts, such as "academic achievement." Knowing how these two concepts are related allows the scientist to use one to say something meaningful about the other.

## Logical Terms

This type of term *relates* the concepts of the statement. Logical terms give declarative statements their form or structure; for example, they can relate concepts in a disjunctive (*either* A *or* B), conjunctive (*both* A *and* B), and conditional (*if* A *then* B) form. Logical terms can also express inverse or direct relationships between concepts. For example, "the more a person talks in a group discussion, the more likely he will be perceived as the leader" expresses a direct relationship between talking and leadership perception. On the other hand, "the more one deviates from the group norm, the less communication will be directed toward him as the group discussion progresses" is an example of an inverse relationship.

Notice that both statements of direct and inverse relationships between concepts can be written in conditional form. For example, "if a person talks a majority of the time in a group discussion, then he is likely to be perceived by others as being the leader" is a statement of conditional form expressing a direct relationship between the two concepts of talking and leadership perception.

An operationally defined concept is conditional in form; *if* a person is given a Stanford-Binet test, *then* his score on the test is taken to be an indicator of intelligence. The "if" clause stipulates the circumstances of the observation (i.e., the particular test instrument to be used or observation strategy to be selected), and the "then" clause stipulates what behavior will count as an instance of the concept (i.e., the test score or the behaviors actually observed).

In short, theoretical statements are characterized both by their form (logical terms) and their content (descriptive terms or concepts). The components of theory, then, are statements that specify logical relationships among concepts. A theory is a system of such statements.

## ANALYTIC AND SYNTHETIC STATEMENTS

There are two fundamentally different types of theoretical statements; synthetic and analytic. *Synthetic statements* are empirical in nature; i.e., they obtain their validity from the actual content being described and synthesized. They are probability statements rather than mathematical or logical statements. For example, the statement, "the more involved a person is in his position, the more difficult it will be to persuade him to change his position" (Sereno, 1969), is synthetic. Terms such as "more" and "less" are statistical or probability terms rather than mathematical or logical. The statement is valid by virtue of its content; we could not replace concepts such as "involved," "position," and "persuade" with symbols such as "A," "B," and "C" in the above statement and still maintain that that statement is true or valid. For example, "the more A a person is in his B, the more difficult it will be to C him to change his B," makes no logical or empirical sense.

*Analytic statements,* on the other hand, are logical in nature. They are true not by virtue of the actual content dealt with but by virtue of their logical form. Analytic statements are said to be valid by definition; they are *tautological.* A syllogism is a good example of an analytic statement; "All men are mortal, Socrates is a man, therefore Socrates is mortal." The statement is equally true when the concepts of "man," "mortality," and "Socrates" are replaced by the symbols "A," "B," and "C." For example, "All A are B, C is A, therefore C is B," does make logical sense.

A theory comprised of analytic statements is assessed in terms of its logical form whereas a theory consisting of synthetic statements is considered valid if its content conforms to existing facts. This property was referred to as the "truth criterion" in Chapter 1. If the statements conform to, and thereby explain, a variety of empirical events they are said to be valid. Theories said to be valid because of their logical form are referred to as *formal theories* whereas those said to be valid because of their empirical correctness are referred to as *substantive theories.*

## DIMENSIONS OF ANALYTIC AND SYNTHETIC STATEMENTS

We will differentiate among theoretical statements along the dimensions of *scope, source,* and *validity.* These same dimensions will highlight how the statements are used differently in formal and substantive theories.

### Scope and Source

The first dimension refers to the scope of a statement; it can be either *specific, general,* or *universal* in its claim. The second dimension refers to the source of a statement; it can be *assumed,* which means it is primary and not reduced in any way from another statement; it can be *inferred* from a primary statement, which means its relation to its parent statement is very loose and speculative; it can be *derived* from a primary statement, which means that the empirical content of the primary statement suggests the secondary statement; or it can be *deduced* from a primary statement, which means that the logical form of the primary statement dictates the logical validity of the secondary statement.

### Validity

The third dimension refers to the validity of the statement. A statement is *tautologically valid* if the primary statement from which it is deduced logically is valid. For example, if we, break apart the syllogism used earlier into three separate statements, the conclusion that "Socrates is mortal" is tautologically valid because it is deduced from the statement "all men are mortal" which is assumed to be valid at the outset.

A statement is *empirically valid* if all concepts in it are subject to observation. For example, the statement, "Lower-class blacks are better educated than upper-class whites," is an empirically valid statement because all of the concepts in it can be defined operationally and therefore observed. Notice that the statement may or may not be empirically true; determination of the empirical truth of a statement depends upon the facts collected. But the statement is empirically valid because it tells us what constitutes facts the aggregate of which can be used to determine the empirical truth of the statement. We can define operationally what blacks and whites are and the number of years of formal education we take to mean better educated and more poorly educated. The questions of validity and truth, then, are separate issues.

A statement is *semantically valid* if only *some* of its component concepts are definable operationally and therefore observable. For example, in his theory of social order Duncan (1968) makes the statement that, "social order is created and sustained in social dramas through intensive and frequent communal presentations of tragic and comic roles whose proper enactment is believed necessary to community survival" (p.60). It is certainly possible to define operationally concepts such as "social order," "social drama," "proper enactment," and "community survival," but there are no commonly acceptable ways of doing so at present. As it stands, the only readily observable concepts in that statement are "tragic role" and "comic role" which role theory research in sociology makes possible.

A statement is *syntactically valid* if none of its concepts can be observed readily and defined operationally. Let's take another of Duncan's statements as an example. "Social order is always a resolution of acceptance, doubt, or rejection of the principles that are believed to guarantee such order" (p.61). The statement contains concepts that potentially could be operationalized but as it stands a social scientist would be in doubt as to what should be observed to establish the truth or falsity of the statement.

## TYPES OF ANALYTIC AND SYNTHETIC STATEMENTS

Gibbs (1967) lists six types of theoretical statements—fact, hypothesis, proposition, postulate, axiom, and theorem—used in consturcting theories. But he does not define each statement-type relative to the type of theory in which it is used. We will add a seventh state-

| Type of statement | Scope of statement | | | Source of statement | | | | Validity of statement | | | |
|---|---|---|---|---|---|---|---|---|---|---|---|
| | Specific | General | Universal | Assumed | Inferred | Derived | Deduced | Syntactical | Semantical | Empirical | Tautological |
| Fact | S | | | S | | | | | | S | |
| Hypothesis | | S | | | | S | | | | S | |
| Proposition | | S | A | S&A | | | | | | S | A |
| Postulate | | S | A | S&A | | | | | S | | A |
| Axiom | | S | A | S&A | | | | S | | | A |
| Theorem | | S | A | | S | | A | | | S | A |
| Law | | | A | | | | A | | | S | A |

Fig. 1. Types of statements used to construct theories defined in terms of the scope, source and validity of statements. S refers to a synthetic statement and A refers to an analytic statement. This figure is a modified illustration of Gibbs's (1967) typology of statements used in theory construction.

ment—law—and define each statement in terms of the type of theory which it is used to construct.

## Fact

Figure 1 is a modification of Gibbs's (1967) tabular illustration of the typology of theoretical statements. A *fact* is a statement applying to a particular time and place (its scope is specific), that is not reduced from another statement (its source is assumed), all of whose concepts are observable (it is empirically valid). "Alphonse Zelditch is highly ego-involved in the general topic of the Watergate Affair," is a statement of fact which is either true or false. The scope of the statement applies only to Alphonse; it did not have to be reduced from another statement, it is either true or false on its own merit; and all of its concepts can be observed. Ego-involvement theory, which we will be discussing later, provides us with the instruments for operationally defining high ego-involvement and we can identify readily Alphonse Zelditch.

## Hypothesis

A *hypothesis* is a statement proposing a relationship between two or more different aggregates of facts. It is general in scope applying to more than one event but it is not universal because it does not claim to cover all events of a given type. It is deduced or derived from another statement or series of statements. For example, ego-involvement theory is based on eight primary statements that are assumed to be ture. From these initial statements and some additional secondary statements, researchers empirically derive hypotheses. "Dyads consisting of slightly involved subjects will reach public agreement with greater frequency than will dyads consisting of subjects who are highly involved" (Sereno and Mortensen, 1969) is a hypothetical statement initially derived from the primary and secondary statements of ego-involvement theory. The relationship between the primary statements and hypotheses will become clearer when we discuss ego-involvement theory in detail later. The important point to keep in mind is that the statement relates aggregates of facts about degree of ego-involvement and aggregates of facts about public agreement. Hypothetical statements are empirically valid insofar as all of the component concepts are operationally definable and therefore observable.

## Law

A statement of *law* is analytic by its very nature. Its scope is universal because it applies to all events of a given class. In physics the laws of thermodynamics are good examples of lawlike statements; they apply to all physical objects. Such statements are deduced logically from other universal lawlike statements. Finally, laws are tautologically valid because it is the form rather than the content of the statement that renders it valid. We will be concerned minimally with statements of law because there are few, if any, statements in the social sciences that are considered universal in scope.

## Proposition

The four remaining types of statements may be either synthetic or analytic depending upon the nature of the theory of which they are a part. A *proposition* statement, whether synthetic or analytic, functions as a primary statement in a theory. In a formal theory an analytic proposition is universal in scope and is tautologically valid. In a substantive theory a proposition is general in scope and empirically valid. To continue with the example of ego-involvement theory as an instance of substantive theory, we said earlier that it consisted of eight primary statements and some secondary statements from which hypotheses were derived. None of these primary statements is a proposition, however, because not all of the concepts in the primary statements of ego-involvement theory are observable. Stated another way, for a primary statement of a theory to be a proposition it must be empirically valid and to be empirically valid all of its component concepts must be observable and operationally definable. In a substantive theory, then, a synthetic proposition must be general in scope, assumed in source, and empirically valid.

## Postulate

A *postulate,* like a proposition, is assumed and functions as a primary statement in a theory. An analytic postulate, like an analytic proposition, is tautologically valid and universal in scope. In a formal theory, then, there is no difference between a propositional and postulational statement; both are universal in scope, assumed in source, and tautologically valid. They have identical functions in formal theories.

You may be wondering why statements with identical theoretical functions are given different names. The reason is that the two types of statements have different functions in substantive theories. A synthetic postulate, like a synthetic proposition, is general in scope and functions as a primary theoretical statement. But a postulate is a "weaker" statement than a proposition in terms of validity because all of the concepts are observable in a proposition whereas only some of the concepts are observable in a postulate.

Consider the first primary statement of ego-involvement theory as an example of a synthetic postulate; "When humans are presented with a message containing one or more positions on one or more topics, they order those positions on a psychological dimension." This statement is assumed and is general in scope. It is semantically rather than empirically valid because only some of its concepts are observable directly. It is possible to define operationally what a "message" is and what "topics" and "positions" are but it is not possible to readily observe what a "psychological dimension" is. There have been several attempts to define that concept so it could be observed, but there is less than widespread agreement about the satisfactoriness of those attempts. In short, propositions are empirically valid whereas postulates are semantically valid.

## Axiom

An *axiom* in a formal theory is identical to a postulate or proposition. Again, the reason for a separate term is not dictated by the requirements of formal theory but of substantive theory. A synthetic axiom, like synthetic postulates and propositions, is a primary statement in a theory. It is assumed at the outset to be true and secondary statements are added to it so that hypotheses eventually can be derived and tested. The difference between a synthetic axiom and synthetic postulates and propositions is that an axiom is the weakest statement-type in terms of validity; none of its component concepts is readily subject to observation.

Recall the discussion of validity in an earlier section when dimensions of analytic and synthetic statements were considered. Duncan's (1968) statement that, "Social order is always a resolution of acceptance, doubt, or rejection of the principles that are believed to guarantee such order" (p.61) was said to be syntactically valid because none of its component concepts is readily observable. That statement would have to be used as a primary statement in a carefully constructed theory and, as such, is a good example of an axiom.

### Theorem

A *theorem,* whether it be in formal or substantive theory, is a secondary statement; propositions, postulates, and axioms are primary statements in a theory. In a formal theory a theorem is a universal statement deduced from a primary statement (which may be called either proposition, postulate, or axiom). Because a deduced statement is analytic, it must be tautologically valid.

In a substantive theory a theorem is inferred or derived rather than deduced from the primary statement(s). A synthetic theorem, like all other synthetic statements, is general in scope. Like a synthetic proposition, a theorem is empirically valid; all of its concepts are observable and operationally definable.

How all of these theoretical statements are combined to result in viable theories is considered in the next section.

## HOW TO CONSTRUCT SUBSTANTIVE THEORIES

Formal theories will be discussed in greater detail in Chapter 9 with respect to their role in model building. For now, it is sufficient to note that formal theories consist of a primary universal statement (or statements), and a theorem (or theorems) deduced from the primary statement(s). The primary universal statements are laws and are called propositions, postulates, or axioms in formal theory construction. These terms have been used frequently as synonyms in substantive theory building as well, resulting in needless confusion. One of the contributions of Gibbs's (1967) typology, although he does not point it out, is that it provides definitions of those terms and differentiates their roles in substantive theory construction. The remainder of this section is devoted to a discussion of substantive theory and how it is constructed using component synthetic statements.

Not just any cluster of synthetic statements is a substantive theory. Care must be taken to identify important properties of statements so the result is a viable theory. Even when statements are combined in proper ways, the result is a temporary conceptualization that never can be proven; theories can be supported or falsified but not proven. It is the task of the scientist to formulate theories in ways that facilitate their own testing. An ambiguous theory may be hard to falsify but it is impossible to support. An untestable theory simply is an unsatisfactory scientific explanation.

### Assuming Primary Statements

A substantive theory is a series of interrelated statements. The statement or statements that begin the series are assumed to be true and are called primary statements. Scientific inquiry is aimed at collecting information to support or falsify, either directly or indirectly, the primary statements. This is essential because primary statements are assumed; they are not reduced from another set of statements. Consequently, secondary statements must be added to the primary statements so that the assumptions can be tested for accuracy.

The fewer the number of statements comprising a theory, the easier it is to test. Theories with relatively few statements in them are said to be more parsimonious than theories with a greater number of statements. The goal of social scientists is to construct the most parsimonious theories of human behavior as is possible. It is possible to construct different types of theories depending upon their degree of parsimony. Subsequent chapters will discuss these different types of theories. For the remainder of this chapter we will discuss the rules that govern the combination of different types of statements that result in viable substantive theory.

### Adding Secondary Statements

Secondary statements can be added to primary statements in several different ways. The only requirements for a primary statement are that its source be assumed and its scope be general; its validity can be empirical, semantical, or syntactical. In other words, propositions, postulates, or axioms can function as primary statements of a substantive theory. This means that for substantive theory not all concepts in the primary statement(s) need be directly observable.

To be testable, however, a substantive theory must contain at least one empirically valid statement that is general in scope (Gibbs, 1967, p.78). This means that if the primary statements are not propositions (recall that propositions are empirically valid but postulates and axioms are not) at least one of the secondary statements must be empirically valid. The only empirically valid statement the source of which is another statement or set of statements is a theorem. In short, if the primary statements of a theory are axioms or postulates, at least one theorem must be added before hypotheses can be derived to test the accuracy of the theory.

The reason it is essential to have at least one empirically valid general statement in a theory is because to be tested, all of the concepts involved must be observable. If concepts cannot be defined operationally it is impossible to conduct a definitive test; there is no way of determining if the results of the test support or falsify the theory. For example, one reason it has been nearly impossible to support or falsify the leading theories of extrasensory-perception phenomena is because no single primary or secondary statement can be made using concepts that are observable and operationally definable. Results of experiments are difficult to interpret because it is uncertain to what parts of the theory results are applicable.

## Deriving Hypotheses

The purpose of constructing a theory is to explain a phenomenon or class of phenomena and to test the accuracy of the theory it is necessary to derive hypotheses from it. Essentially, a hypothesis is a statement that is proposed to be true if the statements from which it was derived are true. Inasmuch as all the concepts in a hypothesis must be observable, all the concepts in the statement(s) from which it is derived must be observable. That is the chief reason why at least one empirically valid statement of general scope must be included in a theory before it can be tested.

Hypotheses can be derived directly from primary statements when those statements are propositions. Hence, theories whose primary statements are propositions are the most parsimonious because they can be tested directly by deriving hypotheses from them. If the primary statements of a theory are postulates, at least one theorem must be inferred from the postulate(s) before hypotheses can be derived. Consequently, a theory the primary statements for which are postulates is less parsimonious than theories whose primary statements are propositions. Theorems are *inferred* from postulates rather than *derived* from them because the relationship between an empirically valid and semantically valid statement is less direct than between two empirically valid statements. Thus, theorems are *inferred* from postulates but hypotheses are *derived* from theorems.

If the primary statements of a theory are axioms, at least two postulates must be *added* to provide at least semantic validity before theorems can be *inferred* to give the theory an empirically valid basis from which hypotheses can be *derived.* A theory whose primary statements are axioms is a theory with no directly observable concepts. As such, nothing can be done with the theory until some semblance of empirical validity is added. This is accomplished usually by adding postulates that, according to the canon of common sense, appear to fit the implications of the axioms.

With postulates the theory has become less parsimonious but it has gained validational respectability; it is now semantically valid. Given that some of the statements of the theory now have some of their component concepts amenable to observation, theorems can be inferred. With the addition of theorems the theory is even less parsimonious but it is now capable of having hypotheses derived from it.

In the case of a theory whose primary statements are axioms, the linkage between primary statement and hypothesis is quite indirect and inferential. Only the theorem(s) from which the hypothesis is derived is tested directly; the postulates which are added to the axioms, as well as the axioms themselves, are tested only indirectly.

A hypothesis, like an operational definition, is conditional in form; it is a statement specifying the necessary conditions of a prediction. *If* the proposition or theorem is true, *then* certain concepts should be observed in specified ways. For example, consider the first proposition of ego-involvement theory; "The more involved in and personally committed to the topic an individual is, the greater is his latitude of rejection and the number of positions on which he remains uncommitted approaches zero." Stated less technically, the proposition asserts that the more committed a person is to a position on a topic, the fewer the positions other than his own he will accept. From this proposition Sereno and Mortensen (1969) derived the following hypothesis; "Dyads consisting of slightly involved subjects will reach public agreement with greater frequency than will dyads consisting of subjects who are highly involved."

The conditional nature of the reasoning behind the derivation of that hypothesis is pretty straightforward and goes as follows. *If* highly ego-involved people accept fewer positions other than the one to which they are committed and *if* we put two people together who are committed to very different positions and instruct them to reach a mutual decision, *then* they should take longer to reach that decision than pairs of people who are willing to accept a wider variety of positions on a given topic (i.e., more slightly ego-involved subjects).

Sereno and Mortensen (1969) conducted an experiment to see if the prediction they made in their hypothesis would be supported or falsified. It was supported. The conclusion is that the proposition from which the hypothesis was derived was supported.

The hypothesis must be an empirically valid statement to determine if the prediction was correct. If the concepts are not defined operationally so that the hypothetical statement can be tested publicly, then it remains unclear whether the results of the observations support or falsify the proposition(s) or theorem(s) under investigation. Stated another way, statements semantically or syntactically valid cannot be used to test propositions or theorems; the statements used for test purposes must be empirically valid. In the strict sense of the term, a prediction is a hypothesis if and only if it is derived from a proposition or theorem.

## Accompanying Facts

A hypothesis cannot be derived from a proposition or theorem alone, however. Two statements of fact must accompany the proposition or theorem; one to initiate the prediction and a second to test it. When a scientist states a fact, he makes a statement describing the instance of a concept. To say, "It is a fact that Clyde is intelligent" is to say that the concept "intelligence" has an instance in the person of Clyde. That statement of fact is said to be "true" if, given an agreed upon operational definition of the concept "intelligence," Clyde obtains a score which is agreed to indicate high intelligence. The statement is "false" if Clyde does not obtain a sufficiently high score. From this point of view, *concepts* are said to be useful, clear, or well-defined but not true or false. A *fact* either is or is not an instance of a concept. A *statement of fact* is either true or false. In short, a fact is an instance of a concept included in a propositional or theorematical statement. The hypothesis is the prediction of a particular relationship among concepts.

It should be apparent by now that factual and hypothetical statements are not integral parts of a theory per se. Rather, they are bridging statements that function to test propositions and theorems directly, and postulates and axioms indirectly. These four synthetic statements are the building blocks of substantive theory. Facts exist independent of general statements that incorporate them, and hypotheses are simply attempts to support or falsify general statements by bridging them to the empirical world. When a hypothesis is supported, it is not incorporated into the theory directly but stands as temporary support for the theory. Theoretical statements assert the generality of facts; hypotheses are predictions that test those assertions. Only the statements asserting generality are part of the theory proper.

*The only reason for formulating a literary theory is the desire to influence critical practice and, subsequently, literature itself. Knowledge that brings about no desirable changes in human behavior is valueless.*

**NORMAN R. F. MAIER AND**
**H. WILLARD RENINGER**
*A Psychological Approach to Literary Criticism*

**4**

# Type I Theory: Burke's Theory of Motives

## INTRODUCTION

In the last chapter it became apparent that theoretical statements can be arranged in different orders resulting in different types of theories. This chapter, and the next three, provide descriptions of the four major types of theories and examples of each. The four examples of theories were chosen because of their assumed familiarity to a communication audience, not because of an assumed theoretical superiority over others.

No pretense is being made to describe these theories in their entirety. You will be introduced to each but for a detailed treatment you will have to look elsewhere. Each theory is described in the following manner. First, the questions behind the theory are discussed. Second, the basic concepts of the theory are defined. Third, when possible, the theoretical statements connecting these concepts are explicated. Fourth, when possible, hypotheses or theorems inferred, derived, or deduced from the theoretical statements are stated. And finally, each theory is assessed in terms of its sufficiency as an example of the type of theory it illustrates.

## CHARACTERISTICS OF TYPE I THEORY

Kenneth Burke's theory of motives is a reasonable example of a Type I Theory. Such theory contains the greatest number of statements; consequently it is said to be the least parsimonious of substantive theories. The primary statements of such theories consist of axioms. Insofar as such theoretical statements contain no directly observable concepts and are therefore only syntactically valid, postulational statements must be *added* to the theory before it can be tested. It is from these semantically valid postulational statements that empirically valid theorems can be *inferred*. Finally, from these theorematical statements hypotheses are *derived* which function to test the adequacy of the theory. At least one hypothesis must be derived from at least one theorem and the results predicted in the hypothesis are compared to at least one factual statement.

The problem involved in testing a Type I Theory is that not even results supporting the hypotheses support the primary axiomatic statements directly. Positive results can be said to support directly the theorem(s) from which the hypotheses were derived and indirectly the postulates from which the theorems were inferred.

But the connection between test results and the primary axiomatic statements is very tenuous.

In studying Burke's theory of motives you should keep in mind that Burke is not presenting his ideas in theory form in the sense we have been discussing. He does not label statements as being axioms, postulates, theorems, etc. In fact, Burke does not seem concerned that his thinking be translated into theory form at all. This is not to say, however, that his thoughts are not amenable to theoretic formulation. Even though Burke is not concerned that his ideas be cast in theory form, they are relatively good examples, when taken collectively, of the literary style of thought and of Type I Theory. It is with these qualifications that we now consider some of Kenneth Burke's writings.

## BURKE'S THEORY OF MOTIVES

Burke's work is extensive and a detailed review of it here is beyond the scope of this short book. To date, he has published two major works of a planned four-volume series; *A Grammar of Motives* (1945) is an original treatment of the grammatical and logical dimensions of language, and *A Rhetoric of Motives* (c1950) discusses the rhetorical, as opposed to the purely logical and/or grammatical, dimensions of language. The remaining two works yet to be published are, *A Symbolic of Motives,* and *On Human Relations* (Burke, 1953, pp.217–218). Burke's theory of motives is his account of the relationship between motives and language. The result is a provocative way of thinking about human communication.

Burke's (1945, c1950, 1953) theory of motives can be thought of also as a philosophy of rhetorical communication. His work is philosophic insofar as it is inquiry into the nature of human communication based on critical rather than empirical methods. His thinking represents a basic theory or *viewpoint;* it takes the form of a system of interrelated principles rather than a set of theoretical statements.

## THEORETICAL QUESTIONS

The basic assumptions underlying Burke's theory are that first, man is more than a rational animal; he is a symbol-using animal and this distinguishes him from other animals. Second, man uses symbols *rhetorically* in communication to create order in his world and to adjust himself to that world. In a sense, then, rhetoric "is the instrument of strife, because it is the means of defending and competing for this order" (Fogarty, 1959, p.56).

The central questions for Burke are really three in number. First, how are language and motives related? Second, how does man use language rhetorically to create his symbolic world? And third, how does man use language to communicate with others to fit himself and his motives into that symbolic world?

## BASIC CONCEPTS

To describe Burke's theory of motives, six concepts are examined. First, the central concept of *motive* is defined. Next, the characteristic of man essential in the use of language—*the negative*—is discussed. Third, the property of language which allows motives to be attributed to behaviors—*ambiguity*—is treated. The next step is to identify the communicative strategy man uses to adjust himself to and influence the shape of his world of motives—the concept of *identification*. *Hierarchy* is the concept Burke uses to describe the result of identification and the attribution of motives. Finally, *pentad* is the tool Burke uses in his study of communication and motives.

### Motive

It is important to differentiate Burke's use of this concept from its more traditional usage. Typically, motive is thought of as a cause for an action; the motive is thought to precede the action. A person is said to behave a particular way *because* he has a certain motivation. In short, motives usually are thought of as causes, and behaviors are thought of as effects.

With Burke, however, the concept of motive is not used as a causal explanation of human behavior but rather as "shorthand terms for situations" (Burke, 1954, pp.29–30). From this viewpoint, language frequently is used to label behavior after it has been enacted. Language fits and adjusts behavior to a symbolically created world. An example is the war hero who says in retrospect that the behavior others now call heroic could as easily be called cowardly if viewed from another perspective. The soldier did not behave in a particular way *because* he was motivated to be a hero. Rather, after his behavior was completed, he and others summarized it by labeling it heroic.

It is the inherent ambiguity of language that makes the study of motives possible. Almost any behavior can be rationalized or justified by appealing to a motive which is a linguistic label for a situation. Burke discusses *pair terms* which allow different, and seemingly contradictory, motives to be ascribed to the same behavior. For example, *national security—self-interest* is a pair term that could be used by Nixon's supporters and critics alike to label the "Watergate Affair." Supporters would say the politicians involved acted *in the name of* national security whereas the critics would say the same men acted *in the name of* self-interest.

These pair terms are the linguistic shorthand used to attribute motives to behavior. Language is ambiguous enough to accommodate almost any action, and it is the attribution of motives to action via communicative behavior in which Burke is interested. "Often, too, the symbol-user will build what Burke calls 'eulogistic and dyslogistic' labels for his acts, that enable him to indulge, whether consciously or not, for himself or for others, in limitless motivational window dressing" (Fogarty, 1959, pp.73–74).

## The Negative

The concepts of the *negative* and *abstraction* are connected intimately in Burke's theory; one cannot be discussed without reference to the other. Much of the material in Chapter 1 regarding man's ability to use symbols and think (or abstract), although not based on Burke directly, is quite similar to his concept of abstraction.

Man is capable of separating experience from language, of using language to recount experiences, and of classifying and collecting events and experiences via language. It is the ability to disengage himself from contemporaneous space and time and to wander forward and backward in time that sets man apart from other animals. Language is the tool he uses to transform signs into symbols and thereby free himself from the specific here-and-now and give himself the license to generalize in the abstract world of thinking.

Burke (1952) says in his essays on the origin of language that meta-symbolizing, or using symbols about symbols themselves, is the highest form of human abstraction. Burke's example of using symbols about symbols, rather than about concrete "things," is *the negative.* "It is Burke's contention that *not* can be conceived, in an idea, and yet one can have no image of it. All the images one has in connection with it are not really its image but images of the real things of which it is the negation" (Fogarty, 1959, p.66). Burke (1952) says, "Though idea and image have become merged in the development of language, the negative provides the instrument for splitting them apart. *For the negative is an idea;* there can be no image of it. *But in imagery there is no negative*" (p. 260).

Man's ability to use the concept of the negative is an example of his ability to "think a pure idea" without any image of the idea per se. Man can think of an automobile when it is not present physically. He does so by recalling the image of an automobile. But man can also think *not* automobile when it is not present. He does so via negative abstraction; he negates the image of an automobile but the negative abstraction itself has no image.

By his very ability to abstract, man uses the negative continuously. Abstracting is the process of selecting, classifying, and generalizing, which involves saying "no" to events and experiences *not* classified together. Burke's concepts of the negative and abstraction are really two sides of the same coin; to abstract is to use the negative to sort and classify, and negation is an impossibility without the ability to abstract.

### Ambiguity

The concept of ambiguity brings rhetorical communication and linguistics very close together (Fogarty, 1959, p.67). For Burke (1945) there are three ways of defining an idea or object; by the ordering of words, by the grammatical function of the linguistic unit, and by expanding the vocabulary (pp.88–89). Every definition consists of two functional units; a substantive unit and an action unit. This is very similar to what a linguist (e.g., Chomsky, 1964) would call a noun phrase and a verb phrase. The substantive unit of a definition not only defines the specific subject but also helps in defining the specific action.

Definition by the order of words operates on the same principle as definition by grammatical function. The substantive and action units of a definition are composed of a series of words. The order in which the words appear define, more or less efficiently and clearly, the specific subject and action. Definitions can be made more specific as the number of words at one's command increases. The more appropriate the words included in a definition, the more precise it becomes.

Think of an idea or object you want to define. Before you start the defining process there is complete ambiguity in the mind of the reader or listener. Your first step is to indicate the subject units (e.g., man, woman, fire, pollution), and the action units (e.g., runs, walks, spreads, diminishes) of the idea. You now describe the particular subject and action by ordering the descriptive words you use. Finally, you may be able to reduce the number of words in your definition by selecting more appropriate words as your vocabulary increases. Definition is a process of elimination; alternative objects and ideas are eliminated until only the correct one remains.

Language, however, is imprecise and no two human beings ever use the same words in identical ways. Burke (1950) discusses four sources of ambiguity resulting from inadequate definitions. A *contextual definition* relates an idea or object to other "things" in the context rather than defining the idea or object itself (p.24). For example, defining a particular chess piece in terms of the pieces immediately adjacent to it would be a contextual definition. Of course, such a definition is only approximate and is of limited use if others are unaware of the context. An attorney basing his defense of a military officer's alleged war crimes on the unique context of the incident will be successful to the extent that he can define not the incident but its context.

*Derivational definition* defines an idea or object neither in terms of its own attributes nor in terms of its context, but in terms of its sources (Burke, c1950, p.26). Because histories of ideas, words, and events evolve along circuitous paths, however, knowing the source of a term often is an inadequate definition of the word in present use. The same is true when persons are treated as sources of ideas. Defining a concept in terms of who uses it frequently results in misleading and incomplete efforts to remove ambiguity.

*Circumference shifting* is aligned closely with contextual definitions; in the former, two people assign different contexts to the same term resulting in ambiguity. For example, when I use the term "office," I assign a context which is quiet, surrounded by books, and filled with classical music and pipe smoke. When a middle-management organizational executive uses the term, he may assign it to a very different context; one in which the noise level is high, phones are ringing constantly, interruptions are commonplace, and frustrations are many. Ambiguity is inevitable because contexts of terms are shifting continuously.

Ambiguity resulting from *scope-reduction-deflection* is similar to context shifting but differs insofar as the former refers to a term being assigned to contexts of different sizes or scopes (Burke, c1950, pp.77–85). The term "capitalism" is defined one way in the context of a particular organization. It may be defined quite differently in terms of a national economy.

Fogarty (1959) is quick to point out that Burke is concerned with the concept of ambiguity not so much because it should be removed. In fact, Burke does not assume that communication can or should be "completely clear." It is the ambiguity of language that enables man to create his own symbolic realities into which he can fit himself. Ambiguity is important because it is man's way of aligning his actions to his motives, and vice versa. "Hence, instead of considering it our task to 'dispose of' any ambiguity by merely disclosing the fact that it is an ambiguity, we rather consider it our task to study and clarify the resources of ambiguity" (Burke, 1945, p.xix).

The differences between this assumption in Burke's theory and the underlying assumption of information theory, the example of a Type IV Theory, are quite clear. Information theory is concerned primarily with reducing ambiguity whereas Burke is interested in explaining how ambiguity is used symbolically.

### Identification

"Burke's identification is really consubstantiality. It means that things or people, different in other ways, may have one common factor in which they are consubstantial or substantially the same" (Fogarty, 1959, p.74). "A doctrine of *consubstantiality,* either explicit or implicit, may be necessary to any way of life. For substance, in the old philosophies, was an *act;* and a way of life is an *acting-together;* and in acting together, men have common sensations, concepts, images, ideas, attitudes that make them *consubstantial*" (Burke, c1950, p.21).

Burke's concept of identification is very similar to the concept of *reference group.* Both refer to belonging to a similar group or sharing a similar set of values or attitudes. Although we may be different in many respects, we share the similarity of being in an academic environment by choice. Academia is our source of identity, belongingness, consubstantiality.

The relationship between rhetorical communication and identification is a straightforward one; ". . . we might well keep it in mind that a speaker persuades an audience by the use of stylistic identifications" (Burke, c1950, p.56). There would be no need for communication or identification if there were no differences among human beings.

Identification, ambiguity, and motive are closely related concepts. In a rhetorical sense, when a speaker identifies with his audience he is assuming ambiguity and using language to create identity to communicate motivational meanings. It is the inherent ambiguities of language that allow for identification to be articulated and motives to be attributed collectively.

## Hierarchy

As will be seen later, Duncan develops Burke's concept of hierarchy in some detail. For its role in Burke's theory of motives, however, suffice it to say that hierarchy refers to man's universal need for a symmetrical and ordered symbolic environment. In terms of social position, there are always superiors, equals, and subordinates. The definition of the hierarchy is a source of perpetual symbolic struggle; i.e., assigning labels, therefore motives, to situations, people, and people's behavior in situations. Man adjusts himself to symbolic hierarchies via the process of identification. He moves up or down the hierarchy by identifying with the relevant symbols of his superiors or subordinates, respectively. The identification process occurs in the way he uses language rhetorically to communicate to himself and others.

## The Pentad

For Burke, the pentad is both a method of inquiry and an instrument used to apply his theory (Fogarty, 1959, p.60). He contends that any human action can be viewed from five perspectives, hence the root *penta*. Burke is convinced that human symbol using behavior must be viewed from different perspectives simultaneously to comprehend fully the behavior. The first perspective is the *scene* or the environment in which the behavior occurs. The *act* is the behavior itself; the human behavior that is being analyzed in terms of its symbolic composition. The *agent* is the third element of the pentad and is treated as the cause of the act. It is the force, usually a person, considered as the initiator of the action. The *agency* is the means or methods by which the act is carried out or manifested. Finally, *purpose* is considered to be the motive assigned to the agent's act.

## CHARACTERISTICS OF BURKE'S THEORY

The metaphor underlying Burke's theory of motives is a dramatistic one. Human behavior is analyzed in a way similar to a play performed on stage. The pentad terms are obviously dramatistic in origin. Burke might have used Lasswell's (1948) journalistic terms: who; what; when; where; and why. But these latter terms do not spring from an appropriate metaphor for Burke's purposes. He wants to do more than report events, making sure to include appropriate details. He wants to analyze the integral connection between a symbolically grounded language and the motives involved. He wants to assess rhetorical communication in terms of its contribution to the creation of a social hierarchy. For Burke, this symbolic analysis is more heuristic if a provocative metaphor is used. In this case, human behavior is conceived of *as if* it were drama.

The second characteristic of this theory, apparent from the pentad concept, is Burke's commitment to dialectical completeness rather than empirical objectivity. Any behavior is partially understood at best if it is not considered from the five universal viewpoints of the pentad. In fact, Burke maintains that for more finely textured analyses, ratios of the five perspectives should be considered. This results in ten, rather than five, viewpoints: act-scene; act-agent; act-agency; act-purpose; scene-agent; scene-agency; scene-purpose; agent-agency; agent-purpose; and agency-purpose. Each ratio of elements serves as a point of dialectical departure.

The language Burke uses to explicate his theory is literary, and as Kaplan (1964) stated earlier, this style tends to be identified with a particular author. Consequently, theories become associated with the men responsible for their initial articulation.

The form of the theory, as it stands now, is discursive rather than referential, derivative, or deductive. The major concepts are discussed by way of example and by way of the other concepts. But

Burke makes no effort to relate his major concepts in theoretical statements and arrange his theoretical statements so they can be validated empirically. There are no propositions, postulates, or axioms stated as such. In this sense, Burke's theory is not testable and is only syntactically or dialectically valid. But the theory of motives is heuristic; it does suggest a wide variety of questions that could be asked and answered empirically if one desired to do so.

There is nothing inherently unempirical about Burke's theory. If you wanted to transform it from a Type I to a Type II or III Theory, you know the appropriate steps to take.

First, at least some of the central concepts would have to be defined operationally so that they could be lifted from the realm of private insight and transplanted in a field of public observability. Second, these operationally defined concepts would have to be related by carefully selected logical terms to form theoretical statements. Third, these statements would have to be sorted out into those which are to be assumed (primary statements) and those which are to be added, inferred, or derived from them (secondary statements). Once theoretical statements are constructed, the procedures and criteria for developing the different types of theories can be followed. As it now stands, however, the reader must assume what for Burke are the primary and secondary statements and must take considerable liberty in operationally defining key concepts.

As you might have guessed, Burke's theory has not prompted much empirical research; it has prompted a good deal of critical research. The reason for so little empirical research is the difficulty of operationalizing Burke's central concepts and, at the same time, being certain that the intent of the theory has not been violated.

*There are local and temporary islands of decreasing entropy in a world in which the entropy as a whole tends to increase, and the existence of these islands enables some of us to assert the existence of progress.*

**NORBERT WIENER**   *The Human Use of Human Beings*

**5**

# Type II Theory: Duncan's Theory of Social Order

## INTRODUCTION

A Type II Theory is more parsimonious than a Type I Theory insofar as it contains fewer theoretical statements but the statements it does contain are more precise and observable. Hugh Duncan's theory of social order is used to illustrate Type II Theory and like Burke's theory, it is not a perfect illustration. Duncan is guilty of using terms such as "postulate" and "axiom" imprecisely and many of his theoretical statements are more like definitions than statements logically relating two or more concepts. Nevertheless, he is taking many of the ideas Burke discusses in his theory and attempting to make them more precise and orderly. At the end of this chapter we will examine what must be done to transform Duncan's theory as it now exists into a more satisfactory Type II Theory.

## CHARACTERISTICS OF TYPE II THEORY

A Type II Theory consists of at least two postulates as the primary statements of the theory. From the postulates, at least one theorem can be inferred from which, in turn, at least one hypothesis can be derived. As in all theories, at least one additional factual statement is used to check the results of the prediction. If the prediction of the hypothesis is borne out, the primary postulates are supported indirectly and the derived theorem is supported directly.

Unlike a Type III Theory, however, negative results in a Type II Theory cannot be interpreted as falsifying the primary statements. They falsify only the statement from which the hypothesis was derived directly. Thus, it is more efficient to test theories if the primary statements are empirically valid because hypotheses can be derived directly and the test of the theory is said to be more direct. But as will become apparent in subsequent chapters, relatively few social science research areas have sufficient information to define operationally all concepts in their primary theoretical statements. Of necessity, in some instances, theory construction must proceed along a more circuitous path.

Duncan (1962, 1968) was influenced markedly by Burke. Duncan's theory of social order is a direct spin-off of Burke's concept of hierarchy. Duncan elaborates, and in many respects clarifies, Burke's writings by articulating his ideas in the form of "postulates" and "axioms." As is true with Burke's theory of motives, relatively few empirical researchers have attempted to operationalize the main concepts of Duncan's theory of social order. Consequently, the theory remains syntactically, and at best semantically, rather than empirically, valid and, as such, is an example of Type II Theory.

## DUNCAN'S THEORY OF SOCIAL ORDER

Duncan's (1962, 1968) theory of social order, like Burke's theory of motives, springs from a dramatistic metaphor. Whereas Burke's metaphor has a literary flavor, Duncan's is more religious in nature. Duncan openly acknowledges the influence on his thinking of Burke, as well as Mead, Freud, Simmel, Malinowski, and Dewey.

Duncan's theory of communication and social order is being examined as an example of a Type II Theory for several reasons. First, it builds on much of Burke's thinking and treating it, as opposed to some other Type II Theory, lends continuity to the discussion. But Duncan is writing in the academic rather than literary style and his acknowledged audience is the social science community whereas Burke's audience is more specifically the literary community. Third, Duncan extracts theoretical statements from his writings. Finally, and most importantly, Duncan provides us with one of the most provocative, but least attended to, grand theories of communication. Although it is not cast in eristic language and all concepts in the theoretical statements are not observable, its heuristic potential is promising.

## THEORETICAL QUESTIONS

Duncan is a sociologist and identifies his theory of social order as being in the symbolic interactionist tradition of Burke, Mead, and Dewey. He takes sharp exception with social scientists whose theories are based on mechanistic metaphors; i.e., theories that conceive of human behavior in mechanical rather than symbolic terms. For Duncan, communicative behavior is primary social data and the symbolic dimension of such behavior should be the primary focus of theoretical interest for social scientists.

Duncan argues that most social science theories assume the existence of psychological, sociological, economic, anthropological, or political reality depending upon one's parent discipline. Man's communicative behavior, to the extent that it is considered important at all, is treated as an epiphenomenon; as a reflection of what "really" exists. Most social scientists are not satisfied with studying what they feel to be superficial behavior; they want to look behind the reflections to study basic phenomena of which communicative behavior is thought to be only a manifestation.

Duncan's position, to the contrary, is that man's communicative behavior, grounded as it is in symbolic language, is both observable and primary data. Rather than communicative behavior reflecting a more fundamental reality, that behavior constitutes reality. It is symbolically grounded communicative behavior that allows us to conceive of economic, psychological, and sociological experience as "real." Whereas most theories assume social integration of human behavior, Duncan contends that a theory must explain "how" this integration takes place through communication.

Duncan's primary question, and the one his theory is designed to answer, is "how does the dramatistic structure [of social acts] function to achieve social integration?" (1968, p. 19). More specifically, "What is involved (for sociological theory) when theatrical analogies are used (such as the familiar social concept of role) for thinking about social relations? What, specifically, is a dramatic model of social relations? What form of drama do we select or create, to explain the social use of symbols? And, finally, what is *social*, as well as dramatic, about it?" (1968, p. 31). What follows is a paraphrasing of the major concepts of Duncan's theory that set out answers to these questions.

## BASIC CONCEPTS

### Symbols and Naming

The answer to his primary question, of how dramatistic structure functions to achieve social integration, is the process of naming (Duncan, 1968, p.21). Duncan says that names are goads to action (p.21). Men enlist in the military and march off to war *in the name of* democracy, communism, the fatherland, or whatever. Students strike universities *in the name of* student rights and representation. Women refuse to do housework *in the name of* women's liberation. In short, most of man's behavior is enacted in the name of some assumed to be relevant symbol. In this respect, Duncan's concept of naming and Burke's concept of motive are very similar. Recall that Burke says one of two pair terms are attributed to behavior as a way of explaining or making sense out of behavior.

The use of symbols in naming is related to beliefs and action in a very direct way. "Symbols, then, create and sustain beliefs in ways of acting because they function as names which signify proper, dubious, or improper ways of expressing relationships" (Duncan, 1968, p.22). By naming, or investing an action with symbolic significance, certain forms of behavior are approved of and other forms discouraged. The behavior enacted is, therefore, symbolic in import insofar as it is an expression of support or defiance of the current social order. It is because of this potential for affirmation or negation of the present social order that gives human behavior its dramatic quality.

## Social Act

Another of Duncan's arguments with most social science theories is that they focus on the *content* of the behavior, or what behavior actually occurred, but ignore the *form* in which the behavior is enacted. For Duncan, a more comprehensive theory must account for both form and content; both the structure and the function of human behavior. As a sociologist, Duncan (1968) is concerned with explaining what he calls *social acts* (pp.16–17). All social acts, or behaviors occurring in societies, have dramatic form or structure and sociological function or content.

For Duncan, the sociological function of the dramatic form of social acts is organizational. Human behavior functions to organize the social world into institutions which it subsequently supports, modifies, and changes (p.22). Furthermore, each social institution attempts to relate its particular symbols of order to the more general or universal symbols of social order. Implied here is that there is constant struggle among institutions (i.e., social structures) for power to define the larger social order making up our society.

## Hierarchy

Duncan's concept of hierarchy is similar to its counterpart in Burke's theory of motives. The social order consists of institutions (sociological content or function) each with its own hierarchy of roles people play (dramatic form or structure) in maintaining or modifying those institutions (via symbolically invested behavior or what Duncan calls *social acts*). Hierarchies comprise relationships among superiors, equals, and subordinates. In every institution, different people may play different roles in different social acts. But in all of society some people are superior to us, some are subordinate to us, and some are equal to us. Duncan (1968) summarizes this concept in the following manner; "Principles of social order are kept alive in the glory of roles we use to sustain positions of superiority, inferiority, and equality in social position" (p. 23).

It is inevitable, however, that there will be conflict among persons playing roles of superiority and inferiority in the hierarchies. Some blacks are demanding an equalitarian role in the hierarchies of economics and politics and some whites are resisting. Some women are demanding roles of equal power in the hierarchies (institutions) of family and economics and some men are resisting. To use Duncan's conceptual language, persons playing subordinate roles are engaging in social acts (naming forms of behavior once deemed inappropriate as now being appropriate) to reorder social hierarchies by reordering the relationships among the roles. This is accomplished by redefining the roles. These redefinitions are attempted by altering both the content and the form or style of one's behavior. By changing the function and form of behavior, the challenger of the existing social order is identifying with the desired social order. Nonviolent student revolutionaries not only modified the content of their usual student behavior, but they changed the form or style of their behavior as well (e.g., the apparent lack of concern for conventional patterns of dress and language).

In the theory of social order, the concepts of form or style and identification are closely related. Recall that Burke's concept of identification referred to consubstantiality or commonness in the midst of diversity. Duncan's point is that people in conflict with the existing social hierarchies create new identifications of commonness via altering their style of behavior and simultaneously investing the new style with symbolic significance with which others playing similar roles can identify.

### Dramatic Form

Duncan's reliance on a dramatistic metaphor is most obvious in his explication of the concept of dramatic form. He conceives of sym-

bols in terms of potency and power. Recall that for him, naming is
a goading force. "Symbols reach their highest state of power in
struggles between good and bad principles of social order as per-
sonified in heroes and villains, Gods and devils, allies and enemies,
and the like. . . . But in the most profound and moving dramas of
social life the 'bad guy' is transformed into a victim whose suffering
and death purges the social order" (Duncan, 1968, p. 23).

The religious flavor of Duncan's dramatistic metaphor is apparent in his description of the behavior process by which social
orders (i.e., hierarchies or institutions) are maintained or modified
over time. A hierarchy comprises a particular ordering of powerful
symbols in the name of which men act. When someone playing an
inferior role perceives himself disfranchised, he wants to play an
equal or superior role. To do so, however, means changing the
social order which, as Duncan maintains, involves a struggle over
symbols; their ordering and their potency. The challenger modifies
the form of his behavior because change in form also results in
change in social function; *"how* we communicate determines *what*
we communicate" (Duncan, 1968, p. 32).

But those playing superior roles in the existing social order see
the attempt at modification as an attempt to defile what is good, just,
and sacred. So for those in control of the powerful symbols, a way
must be found to purge the hierarchy of the challenger and keep the
social order pure. "Symbols are kept pure through victimage or
sacrifice" (Duncan, 1968, p. 23). If those controlling the symbolic
order are unsuccessful, those new in the role of superiority conse-
crate the new social order by purging those formerly in power. If
the challengers are unsuccessful, they become victims of the purge
to reconsecrate the existing social order. "All social order depends
on consecration through communication" (Duncan, 1968, p. 23).

## Rules

The concept of rule is an important one for Duncan for several
reasons. First, rule influences every form of social behavior and,
"unlike tradition, law, or the dark mysteries of religion, never de-
rives its power from appeals to a sacred or supernatural source"
(Duncan, 1968, p. 36). Rules are the product of implicit or explicit
cooperation among persons for whom the rules pertain. Because
rules are thought to be less rigid than traditions and laws, they can

be changed by agreement among those affected in the process of informal communication.

The second reason for the importance of rules is that they derive their power from their form rather than their content per se (Duncan, 1968, p. 37). This is consistent with his argument that the form of behavior determines its function. He contends that it is more important to know the form of a social rule than what the rule actually is. Furthermore, rules are present in all social functions. "For Americans rules are a form of authority, and their study must not be limited to their application in play (important as this is) but to their general use in social action" (Duncan, 1968, p. 39).

## THEORETICAL STATEMENTS

Unlike Burke, who discusses his major concepts but does not cast them into theoretical statements, Duncan does formulate theoretical statements. But Duncan's identification of different types of theoretical statements is an example of the terminological confusion in the social sciences regarding theory construction. Duncan identifies three different types of statements; axiomatic propositions, theoretical propositions, and methodological propositions. Roughly translated into the terminology set forth in Chapter 3, they are postulational and axiomatic statements (replacing the terms axiomatic propositions and theoretical propositions), and methodological guidelines (replacing the term methodological propositions).

Duncan's theoretical statements are not propositions because not all of their constituent concepts are observable. They do vary in their specificity, however, and so can be labeled either postulates or axioms. It is difficult to see any differences in form between what he calls his "axiomatic propositions" and his "theoretical propositions."

Duncan's thirty-six theoretical statements are listed below. No discussion of them individually is offered; for that purpose you should consult the primary source. The reason for listing them here is both to provide examples of theoretical statements comprised of basic concepts and to give you a more complete picture of this theory of social order. All the following statements are taken from *Symbols in Society* (Duncan, 1968).

## Postulates and Axioms

1.   Society arises in, and continues to exist through, the communication of significant symbols (p.44).

2.   Man creates the significant symbols he uses in communication (p.47).

3.   Emotions, as well as thought and will, are learned in communication (p.47).

4.   Symbols affect social motives by determining the forms in which the contents of relationships can be expressed (p.48).

5.   From a sociological view motives must be understood as man's need for social relationships (p.49).

6.   Symbols are directly observable data of meaning in social relationships (p.50).

7.   Social order is expressed through hierarchies which differentiate men into ranks, classes, and status groups, and, at the same time, resolve differentiation through appeals to principles of order which transcend those upon which differentiation is based (p.51).

8.   Hierarchy is expressed through the symbolization of superiority, inferiority, and equality, and of passage from one to the other (p.52).

9.   Hierarchy functions through persuasion, which takes the form of courtship in social relationships (p.53).

10.   The expression of hierarchy is best conceived through forms of drama which are *both* comic *and* tragic (p.59).

11.   Social order is created *and* sustained in social dramas through intensive and frequent communal presentations of tragic and comic roles whose proper enactment is believed necessary to community survival (p.60).

12.   Social order is always a resolution of acceptance, doubt, or rejection of the principles that are believed to guarantee such order (p.61).

13.   Social order, and its expression through hierarchy, is a social drama in which actors struggle to uphold, destroy, or change principles of order which are believed "necessary" to social integration (p.63).

14.  Social differences are resolved through appeals to principles of social order believed to be ultimate and transcendent sources of order (p.66).

15.  The structure of social action involves five elements; (1) the stage or situation in which the act takes place; (2) the kind of act considered appropriate to upholding order in group life; (3) the social roles which embody social functions; (4) the means of expression used in the act; (5) the ends, goals, or values which are believed to create and sustain social order (p.67).

16.  All explanations which ground social order in "conditions," "environments," "the body," "forces," or "equilibrium," are situational explanations (p.70).

17.  Social institutions are the most directly observable units of action in society. Eleven such basic units may be distinguished: these are (1) the family, (2) government, (3) economic institutions, (4) defense, (5) education, (6) manners and etiquette (pure forms of sociability), (7) entertainment, (8) health and welfare, (9) religion, (10) art, (11) science and technology (p.71).

18.  In analyzing social roles we ask: what function is supposed to be performed in what role, and how is this role played before various audiences? What style of life is involved in role enactment, and how is this style used to legitimize beliefs in certain forms of social order? (p.72).

19.  Symbolic means of expression, the media in which we express ourselves, must be analyzed for their effect on what we communicate (p.72).

20.  Social action cannot be analyzed solely in terms of situation, institution, role, means of expression, or beliefs in certain principles of social order, but only in a synthesis of all five elements (p.74).

21.  Superiors, inferiors, and equals must expect disobedience, indifference, and disloyalty, and while those who control social order must teach us to feel guilt over the commission of such hierarchical "sins," they must also provide us with way of ridding ourselves of fear and guilt, so that we can act with confidence in the efficacy of the principles of social order under whose name we act (p.75).

22.  All hierarchies function through a "perfection" of their princi-

ples in final moments of social mystification which are reached by mounting from lower to higher principles of social order (p.78).

23.   Five types of audiences are addressed in social courtship: these are, first, general publics ("They"); second, community guardians ("We"); third, others significant to us as friends and confidants with whom we talk intimately ("Thou"); fourth, the selves we address inwardly in soliloquy (the "I" talking to the "Me"); and fifth, ideal audiences whom we address as ultimate sources of social order ("It") (p.81).

24.   The general public ("They") is a symbolization of the whole community (p.93).

25.   The community guardians ("We") symbolize the conscience of the community (p.95).

26.   The significant other ("Thou") is symbolized through dialogue in which the self is created and sustained (p.100).

27.   Soliloquy, like inner dialogue between the "I" and the "Me," is the symbolization of role conflict in society (p.105).

28.   Principles of social order are grounded in ultimate principles of order which serve as the final audience in social address (p.110).

29.   Social order is legitimized through symbols grounded in nature, man, society, language, or God (p.116).

30.   Social order, and its expression through hierarchy, is enacted in social dramas in which actors attempt to uphold, destroy, or change the principles of that social order (p.123).

31.   Hierarchical communication is a form of address (courtship) among superiors, inferiors, and equals (p.127).

32.   Disorder in society originates in disorder in communication (p.130).

33.   Social disorder and counter-order arise in guilt which originates in disobedience of those whose commandments are believed necessary to social order (p.135).

34.   Society must provide us with means to expiate guilt arising from sins of disobedience (p.140).

35.   Victimage is the basic form of expiation in the communication of social order (p.144).

36.   Victimage of the self is determined by social victimage (p.147).

## CHARACTERISTICS OF DUNCAN'S THEORY OF SOCIAL ORDER

Although Duncan's theory, like Burke's theory of motives, springs from the same metaphorical ground, the two theories are cast in different languages. Duncan clearly sets himself apart from social scientists who build their theories from mechanistic metaphors. He demonstrates the importance many scientists ascribe consciously to the metaphors which generate their theories. Duncan's argument is as much on aesthetic as epistemological grounds. If man is a symbol user, how can we think of man as a machine that gears and meshes with others? That is an inconsistency Duncan tries to resolve in his theory.

The language of Duncan's theory is more academic in style than Burke's, but the form of his theory is discursive. There is no inferential or derivative reason for the order in which Duncan presents his theoretical statements. He does not attempt to infer or derive more specific statements from his set of thirty-six. He is writing for a social science audience and yet is not concerned particularly to have other scientists test his theory. Rather, he seems to be arguing for the acceptance of his metaphor and the thirty-six assumptions his theory makes.

Consider statements 1, 2, 3, 5, 6, 8, 13, 15, 16, 17, 22, 23, 24, 25, 26, 27, 31, and 34. These statements can be best thought of either as definitions or as statements which must be assumed because there is no readily apparent way of testing them. Stated in the vocabulary we have developed, these statements are primary; some of them are axioms and some are postulates. Axiomatic statements have no readily observable concepts in them and postulational statements have some observable concepts. For example, statement 3 could be considered a postulate insofar as psychologists have developed various paper-and-pencil as well as direct observational instruments which define emotional states. Any one of several operational definitions of communication could be used as a means of observing that concept directly. On the other hand, statement 6 is an example of an axiom insofar as Duncan is vague about what he means by "symbol," "meaning," and "social relationships." These terms can be defined operationally, but Duncan provides no guidelines for assessing the correctness of such attempts.

With the exception of statements 18 through 20, which are really strong suggestions for how to conduct research, the remainder of the statements express relationships among concepts to varying degrees of satisfaction. Missing from all of these statements, however, is any indication of the strength or in some instances the direction of the relationships. Consider statement 7 for example; social order and social differentiation are said to be related. In addition, social order and difference resolution are said to be related vis-à-vis appeals to principles of order.

The difficulty with this statement is that the concepts being related are not defined adequately and the strength and direction of the relationship is left unspecified. We do not know if the relationship between social order and social differentiation is direct (the more social order in existence, the more social differentation will be observed) or inverse (the more social order in existence, the less social differentiation will be observed). In addition, we do not know what "social order," "social differentiation," "hierarchies," and "principles" are; we do not know what to observe to see instances of these concepts.

Nevertheless, this latter class of statements could be phrased as research questions or, when properly defined and constructed, treated as hypotheses. It is not impossible to re-order Duncan's statements into primary and secondary categories, propose more adequate definitions of key concepts, derive some hypotheses and thereby test the adequacy of the theory. As it stands, however, it needs considerable work before the adequacy of this theory could be determined. But Duncan has gone further than did Burke in identifying key statements which constitute the theory of social order.

As it stands, Duncan's theory is syntactically valid; he makes little effort to define operationally his basic concepts. But it does differ from Burke's theory insofar as Duncan has articulated a set of primary statements. It remains for others, however, to develop and test it. Theorems must be inferred from the set of primary statements and then hypotheses derived and tested if the theory is to achieve empirical validity.

*. . . the act of knowing includes an appraisal; and
this personal coefficient, which shapes all factual
knowledge, bridges in doing so the disjunction between
subjectivity and objectivity.*

**MICHAEL POLANYI**    *Personal Knowledge*

**6**

# Type III Theory:
# Ego-Involvement
# Theory

# INTRODUCTION

The theory of ego-involvement is a Type III Theory. Ego-involvement is one of several approaches to a more general theory of attitude-change. Because Type III Theory is cast in eristic rather than literary or academic language, it is less identified as the work of one particular scholar, as was the case with the examples of Type I and II Theories. However, the communication scientists who have contributed both empirical data and theoretical formulations have been Sherif, Sherif, and Nebergall (1965), Sereno (1968), Sereno and Mortensen (1969, 1970), Wilmot (1971), and Sereno and Bodaken (1972). Warranted assertions that began as derived hypotheses have been incorporated into the theory as new postulates or propositions as they gained empirical support.

As was the case with the examples for the preceding two types of theory, ego-involvement theory is not a perfect illustration of Type III Theory. Those responsible for its development have not conscientiously labeled statements as propositions, postulates, or theorems. Consequently, I have taken the liberty of arranging the theoretical statements comprising ego-involvement theory into the categories developed in this book. The fit is not perfect; consequently, the steps needed to transform ego-involvement theory into a more accurate illustration of Type III Theory are discussed at the end of this chapter.

# CHARACTERISTICS OF TYPE III THEORY

A *Type III Theory* is the most parsimonious substantive theory; at least one proposition functions as the primary statement and, coupled with at least one factual statement, a hypothetical statement is derived. The results of the test are related back to at least one other factual statement, thus fulfilling the bridging function of a hypothesis. If the factual statement corroborates the test results, the propositional statement is said to be supported directly and the "truth criterion" satisfied. A Type III Theory, then, consists of at least one propositional statement from which at least one hypothetical statement can be derived. Inferential steps are eliminated.

## EGO-INVOLVEMENT THEORY

The subtitle of ego-involvement theory—a social judgment approach to attitude theory—is helpful in several respects. First, the concept of attitude has been one of the most widely used and researched ideas in the social sciences. The subtitle indicates a specific, and relatively recent, theoretical effort to explain attitudes and their changes. Second, the subtitle refers to the metaphor from which the theory grew. Unlike the theories of motive and social order, which rest on dramatistic metaphors, ego-involvement theory rests on a psychophysical metaphor.

Psychophysical measurement theory has been concerned traditionally with the five human senses and how we make comparative judgments using those senses. For example, studies are conducted to determine how humans judge the relative weights of a series of metal blocks, all of the same size but of different actual weights. Or subjects are presented with a series of objects differing in absolute temperatures and are asked to judge the comparative temperatures of two objects at a time. Another example is presenting subjects with a series of lights and asking them to determine which of the pairs of lights presented is brighter.

Psychophysical measurement theory is interested in explaining the human judgment process involving physical stimuli. Ego-involvement theory uses the primary theoretical statements of psychophysical judgment theory as its metaphorical springboard; it adapts them as its own propositions. Instead of being concerned with psychophysical judgments, the propositions are now applied to social judgments.

## THEORETICAL QUESTIONS

Like the theories of motive and social order, ego-involvement theory is concerned with explaining how communication functions to influence the way man sees the world. The scope of ego-involvement theory, however, is more delimited than the scope of the other two theories. Ego-involvement theory is an attempt to explain why different people receiving an identical message change their attitudes to different degrees. The general answer the theory advances is that some people are more involved in the topic than others; the topic is more salient to some than to others. In Burke and Duncan's terms, the listeners' degree of identification with the issue differs.

Ego-involvement theory assumes that a change in attitudes is a two-step process. First, when we are presented with a persuasive message we make a judgment about the position or extremity of the position of the topic(s) presented relative to our own position. Second, the extent to which we change our attitude after receiving the message is dependent upon the discrepancy we judge to exist between our position on the topic and the position advocated in the message.

## BASIC CONCEPTS

### Ego

Perhaps the central concept in ego-involvement theory is ego. The concept has undergone many changes, some subtle and some radical, from the days of its Freudian inception. We will be considering it as it has become defined in the social science community. Hofling (1967) says, "The ego . . . has been formed as a result of interaction with the environment. . . . (the ego) functions as a boundary to the mind . . . (and) has a regulatory function, determining what stimuli and materials from the environment are to be admitted within the human organism. Similarly, it determines what products are to be allowed to find their way out into the environment, i.e., it regulates what the person says and does. . . ." (p.149).

From this description, which is relatively widely accepted, the ego is conceived of as an intrapersonal gatekeeper. It is a hypothetical construct. That is to say, the ego does not reside at some place within our bodies. Rather, it is an idea created that helps scientists explain human behavior; in this instance, the behavior of attitude change. The ego is a screening device which admits certain stimuli to be perceived and processed and turns away other stimuli because, for any number of reasons, the individual cannot effectively process them. The ego also screens what goes out from the individual. It influences the behavior enacted during everyday, routine living.

Such a conception of ego makes it a very central part of a human being. Sherif and Sherif (1967) have a complementary view of the ego. "Our major psychological activities—our perception, judgment, remembering, and so on—take place in referential frameworks. The ego is no exception to this general rule. We learn (or sometimes determine) what values, goals, standards, or norms are desirable for us. These become incorporated as *our* values, *our* goals. The referential framework of the ego is therefore these values, goals, standards, or norms which have become our major attitudes, which have become so large a part of what we refer to as *me*" (p.114).

## Ego-involvement

Sereno (1969) provides a clear and widely accepted definition of ego-involvement; it "refers to the relevance, significance, and meaningfulness of the issue or topic to the individual. It reveals itself through a person's commitments or stands on the issue" (p.70). From a communication perspective, it is assumed that we are confronted constantly with all types of messages; from television advertisements to informal discussions to presidential appeals. The effectiveness of these messages is mediated, and in part determined, by the ego; the message must be processed by the ego before any attitude change can occur. Putting the matter simply, the position advocated in the message interacts with the position reflected by the ego. Depending upon the nature of the interaction, attitudes change accordingly.

## Latitudes

The goal of ego-involvement theory is to specify all the complexities of the interactions between the message and the ego. Unlike many previous theories of attitude and attitude change, ego-involvement theory contends that a person's attitude cannot be thought of simply as a point on a continuum. If we assume that attitudes toward communism fall along a line from extremely favorable to extremely unfavorable, one person's attitude cannot be thought of as a single point on that line. It is more realistic to assume that a person's attitude occupies a *range rather than a point* on the line. Sherif, Sherif, and Nebergall (1965) were instrumental in operationalizing this conception of attitude. They say, "An individual's attitude on an issue can be assessed adequately only if the procedures yield the limits of the positions he accepts (latitude of acceptance) and the limits of the positions he rejects (latitude of rejection), relative to the bounds of available alternatives defined by the extreme positions on the issue" (p.24).

Operationally defined, the *latitude of acceptance* is "the position on an issue (or toward an object) that is most acceptable, plus other acceptable positions" (Sherif, Sherif, and Nebergall, 1965, p.24). A *latitude of rejection* is "the most objectionable position on the same issue, plus other objectionable positions" (p.24). A *latitude of noncommitment* is defined as "those positions not categorized as either acceptable or objectionable in some degree" (p.24).

A person's attitude can fall in one of three regions. The concepts of latitude originally were defined operationally by what Sherif, Sherif, and Nebergall (1965) called the "Own Category" procedure. This was a procedure by which a person ordered statements in terms of how much he agreed or disagreed with them, and from these orderings his attitudes were inferred. Later, other procedures have replaced the "Own Category" technique (for example, a variation on the semantic differential technique and a procedure Diab devised).

## THEORETICAL STATEMENTS

Inasmuch as ego-involvement theory is cast in eristic language and possesses the other properties of a Type III Theory, the primary statements of the theory are propositions. However, psychophysical measurement theory is translated into social judgment terminology before the propositional statements are articulated. Ideally the theory functioning as the analogue for a new theory would be translated directly into primary statements, preferrably propositional statements. But in the case of ego-involvement theory, Sherif, Sherif, and Nebergall (1965) make a general translation first from which propositional statements are extracted. For this reason the theory is not as parsimonious as it could be.

It should be noted in passing that Sherif, Sherif, and Nebergall (1965) did not identify the stages of their translation process; consequently, the primary statements extrapolated from the general translation are not labeled propositions but are referred to as assumptions or assertions.

## Translating Psychophysical Measurement Theory

As Sherif, Sherif, and Nebergall see it, psychophysical measurement theory yields six general statements about social-judgment which, in turn, can be translated into eight propositional statements for ego-involvement theory.

1.   When humans are presented with a message containing one or more positions on one or more topics, they order those positions on a psychological dimension. This ordering process occurs even when no such instructions are given and when there are no clear standards for such ordering.

2.   To the extent that standards for ordering topics are absent, the orderings will be less stable over time. For example, if we hear a speech advocating a position on a topic of which we know very little, we will have no way of judging how extreme the position being advocated really is. In such cases, we will still order that position on a psychological dimension but it will be less stable (i.e., more easiy changed) than if we had a clear standard for judging the extremity of the position. As we obtain more information on the topic, we have a basis for comparing that initial position, and its ordering may or may not be changed. But its position on the psychological dimension becomes more stable.

3.   Factors such as motivation, learning, contextual effects, and instructional guides influence or distort the social judgments we make about positions on topics being advocated. The influence of these factors is greater when we do not have explicit standards by which to judge positions. When we have very little basis of comparison for a position being advocated, we tend to rely on internal and external factors to assist us in making our social judgments on those positions.

4.   We use the most extreme position being advocated as an anchor or reference point for ordering the other positions advocated in other messages. The most extreme position being advocated will be used as an anchor to a greater extent (a) when we have very little information with which to judge the positions, (b) when all the other positions are not yet known, (c) or when there are no other standards of comparison.

5.   If an anchor position is added that is just slightly more extreme than the most extreme position in existence, there is a tendency for us to judge all of the previously known positions as being slightly more extreme than we did initially. An anchor position only slightly more extreme than the most extreme position functions to assimilate the other positions.

6.   If we place a new position far beyond the previously existing most extreme position, the previous range of positions will be judged as being slightly less extreme than they were initially. An anchor position significantly more extreme than the most extreme previous position functions to contrast the other positions.

## Propositions

From these six general statements Sherif, Sherif, and Nebergall assumed eight propositions to serve as the primary statements of ego-involvement theory.

1.   The more involved in and personally committed to the topic an individual is, the greater is his latitude of rejection and the number of positions on which he remains uncommitted approaches zero.

2.   Less involved individuals are noncommittal toward more positions in the universe of discourse, and their latitudes of acceptance and rejection are approximately equal or encompass equally small segments of the total range of positions on the topic.

3.   The more an individual is personally involved in the topic, the more his own stand serves as an anchor for his appraisals of the message.

4.   The less the position of a message on a topic diverges from the latitude of acceptance, the more the message will be assimilated.

5.   The more the position of a message diverges from an individual's latitude of rejection, the more the message will be contrasted.

6.   The greater the individual's involvement in an issue, the smaller his latitude of noncommitment.

7.   The lower an individual's commitment and the higher the ambiguity level of the topic, the greater the range of assimilation.

For example, the number of alternative positions that can be envisaged feasibly on the topic and within given segments, particularly in the latitude of noncommitment, will vary in direct proportion to the clarity of the topic. With less than the extreme degree of ego-involvement just related, the assimilation range is increased to the extent that the object of the message is unstructured or the communicator can present additional alternatives not within the latitude of rejection.

8.  Attitude change is a function of how an individual categorizes a message and its source (pp.14–16).

## Hypotheses

From these eight propositions, seven hypotheses have been derived, tested, and supported. Sereno and Mortensen (1969) derived several hypotheses regarding dyadic decision-making and ego-involvement. Four of them received support.

1.  Dyads consisting of slightly involved subjects will reach public agreement with greater frequency than will dyads consisting of subjects who are highly involved.

2.  Dyads consisting of slightly involved subjects will exhibit greater changes between private pretest and posttest responses than will subjects who are highly involved.

3.  The frequency of public agreement and the degree of attitude change is a function of involvement in the topic.

4.  As the magnitude of discrepancy becomes larger, there will be greater differences between highly and slightly involved subjects' perceptions of credibility, predispositions toward communication, and the expectations of outcome.

Sereno (1968) derived two hypotheses from ego-involvement theorems regarding the credibility of the source of messages. They were both supported.

5.  If attributed to a highly credible source, highly involved subjects change their attitudes on the topic in the direction advocated less than lowly involved subjects.

6.  When discrepant messages are attributed to a highly credible source, highly involved subjects lower their evaluations of the source more than lowly involved subjects.

7. When presented with a belief-discrepant message, highly involved subjects will demonstrate a decrease in their latitude of rejection. This is the most recently derived hypothesis Sereno and Bodaken (1972) tested.

7a. When presented with a belief-discrepant message, highly involved subjects will demonstrate an increase in their latitude of acceptance.

7b. When presented with a belief-discrepant message, highly involved subjects will demonstrate an increase in the latitude of noncommitment.

## CHARACTERISTICS OF EGO-INVOLVEMENT THEORY

Ego-involvement theory is a good example of the eristic style of thinking that results in research carried out via experimental methods. This is a more middle-range theory than Burke's or Duncan's, which were both grander in scope. The grander theories reflect the intensional growth of knowledge; broad parameters define the territory and eventually the scope of the research the theory generates becomes more focused. Middle-range theories, like ego-involvement theory, begin with a more delimited territory and expand by inferring theorems and deriving hypotheses that extend the scope of our knowledge claims.

As mentioned earlier, the metaphor underlying ego-involvement theory is psychophysical rather than dramatistic. Interestingly enough, however, all three theories are trying to explain how rhetorical communication functions to persuade (change the attitudes of) others. Yet the scope, metaphorical bases, and styles of thought differ noticeably. It has been fairly common in the social sciences to rely on physical or mechanistic metaphors for theories cast in eristic language. The reason is understandable; to date it has been easier to operationalize mechanistic concepts than it has been to operationalize dramatistic ones. This is an important concern for eristically oriented theorists because they strive for empirically valid explanations.

Ego-involvement theory has not evolved in as orderly a manner as implied in this discussion of it. As is frequently the case with

Type III Theories, an argument is made for a point of view resulting from an underlying metaphor. In the case of ego-involvement theory, Sherif, Sherif, and Nebergall (1965) argued that social judgment should have many of the same properties of psychophysical judgment. If the primary statements are true (which, incidentally, are identified very infrequently as postulates or propositions in Type III Theory), then certain conditions should be true. The assumptions are tested by deriving hypotheses, which are usually labeled as such. In short, the statements of ego-involvement theory are classified here according to the typology developed. These theoretical statements are good examples of synthetic propositions, whether the theorists label them as such or not.

It should be noted also that ego-involvement theory, like many social science theories, is not extremely parsimonious although it is moreso than Type I or Type II Theories. There are as many assumed propositions as there are derived hypotheses. An indication of a parsimonious and heuristic theory is one with few primary statements which, in turn, generate a large number of secondary statements.

*Yet the more surely and vividly you know the future,*
*the more it makes sense to say that you've already*
*had it. When the outcome of a game is certain, we*
*call it quits and begin another. . . . the more surely*
*the future is known, the less surprise and the less fun*
*in living it.*

ALAN W. WATTS    *The Book*

**7**

# Type IV Theory: Information Theory

## INTRODUCTION

Information theory is discussed in this chapter as an example of a Type IV Theory. Information theory is the result of work by engineers and mathematicians but stated in its most general form by Shannon and Weaver (1949). It is cast in postulational language (Kaplan's use of that term) and is recognized as a formal rather than substantive theory. Recall that in its simplest form a formal theory consists of at least one analytic primary statement (proposition, postulate, or axiom) from which at least one analytic theorem can be deduced. Information theory consists of five primary statements from which twenty-three theorems are deduced. These theorems are said to be valid not on the basis of empirical testing but on the basis of logical deduction.

Shannon and Weaver's 1964 mathematical theory of communication, which also is referred to as information theory, consists of five primary analytic statements (propositions, postulates, or axioms) and twenty-three deduced theorems. These primary and secondary statements will not be presented here for two reasons. First, considerable space would be required to trace the derivations of the mathematical equations from the primary statements to the theorems. Mathematical language is extremely concise and, for all practical purpose, the result would be the theory as Shannon and Weaver presented it initially. For such a detailed account of the theory, the original source should be consulted.

The second reason is that much of the audience for whom this book is intended does not have sufficient mathematical training to benefit sufficiently from such a detailed account of the theory. There are other sources to consult for a nonmathematical translation of the theory (e.g., Pierce, 1961). The strategy of this chapter is to present an introduction to information theory by way of a discussion of its basic concepts.

## INFORMATION THEORY

Human communication is recognized to have three dimensions; the syntactic, the pragmatic, and the semantic dimensions. If you study the *syntactic dimension* of communication you are interested in the relation of signals, functioning as signs, to other signals, also functioning as signs. If you are interested in the *semantic dimension* you study the relation of signals, functioning as symbols, and their referents. If you work on the *pragmatic dimension* of communication you ask how signals, functioning either as signs or symbols, are related to human behaviors.

The syntactic dimension is concerned with *structural* meaning; signals are treated as signs which denote but do not connote. The semantic dimension is concerned with *symbolic* meaning; the signals are treated as symbols that have both denotative and connotative powers. The pragmatic dimension is concerned with *behavioral* meaning; the concern is with how signals, treated either as signs or symbols, influence human behaviors.

The theory of motives and the theory of social order can be thought of as theories of the semantic dimension of communication. Their emphasis is on how symbols mean what they do to human beings. The theory of ego-involvement is primarily, although not exclusively, a theory of the pragmatic dimension; how do signs and symbols influence attitudinal behavior. Information theory, which we are about to consider, is a theory of the syntactic dimension. Its primary concern is with how signals, treated as signs, are related to other signs.

## THEORETICAL QUESTIONS

In 1924, Nyquist, who at that time was a mathematician working for AT&T, was trying to clarify the relationships between the speed of telegraphy and corresponding current values. The concern of AT&T was how to send telegraphic messages as efficiently as possible. In 1928, Hartley elaborated on Nyquist's work by introducing and defining the concept of a message-sender. For Hartley, a message-sender was any device that had before it a pool of signals. The device could select various combinations of signals from the pool to send coded messages. The goal, again, was to make telegraphic communication as efficient as possible. Shannon and Weaver followed up on the work of Nyquist and Hartley and in 1949 published two papers jointly referred to as *The Mathematical Theory of Communication.*

The central question Shannon and Weaver were trying to answer was how messages could be encoded into signals most efficiently and how those signals could be transmitted with minimum error over a channel or circuit of a given capacity. To answer this general question, they had to discover a way of quantifying information so they could determine the efficiency of its transmission. They also had to determine a method of specifying what the capacity of a channel was for transmitting encoded messages. They had to devise a method for encoding messages into the fewest number of signals possible. And finally, they had to assess the effects of noise or distortion in the channel on the encoded message being transmitted.

Figure 2 illustrates graphically the communication process to which Shannon and Weaver's theory applies. Let's use the example of a telegram being sent to explain the figure. A telegrapher is given a message to be sent which is written out in the English language. He first must encode that message into Morse, which is the pool of signals available. The telegrapher then uses his telegraph key device to transmit the encoded message, which is now a series of dots and dashes. The message is transmitted over a telegraph wire, which is the channel. The wire has a certain capacity for handling messages. Only a certain number of signals can be sent at any one time and these signals can be sent at a certain rate. There is, however, inevita-

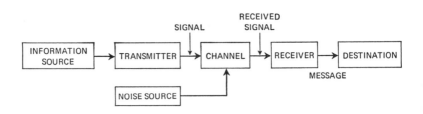

**Fig. 2** Communication systems may be reduced to these fundamental elements. In telephony the signal is of varying electric current, and the channel is a wire. In speech the signal is varying sound pressures, and the channel the air. Frequently things not intended by the information source are impressed in the signal. The static of radio is one example; distortion in telephony is another. All these additions may be called noise. (Reprinted from Warren Weaver. The mathematics of communication. *Scientific American* **181**, p. 12.)

ble noise, static, or distortion in the channel. This noise disrupts the message being transmitted by affecting the clarity with which it is received at its destination. The encoded message is received by an appropriate electromechanical device and the information destination, usually another telegraph operator, decodes the message back into the English language.

## BASIC CONCEPTS

### Information

The concept of information, as Shannon and Weaver use the term, is not at all like the common meaning of information. Information usually is synonymous with content; a book or newspaper is said to contain content or information. But in information theory the concept of information has a technical definition. *It refers not to the content contained in a message but to all the possible messages that could be transmitted.* In this respect, the concept of information is aligned closely with the concept of uncertainty.

Perhaps an example will help to clarify. Assume you are a secret agent and you receive all of your instructions in code from an anonymous source. You know when you are to receive these messages, but you have no idea what the instructions will be. You do know, however, that the messages will be encoded using different combinations and sequences of eight numbers. In short, the source has available to him eight different signals he can use to encode your instructions.

Assume that I, too, am a secret agent in the same operation except I know that my source encodes my instructions using only two numbers. For the purpose of this example, assume that the signals (i.e., numbers) in the two codes are independent and equally probable. This means that the sender can select any number without being constrained by that choice in selecting the next number.

Information theory says that your message, encoded with eight numbers, conveyed more information than does my message encoded with only two numbers. Why? Because each number in your message reduced more uncertainty for you than did the numbers in my message. You knew that each number in your message could be followed by any one of eight numbers. In guessing what the next number would be, you had only a one-in-eight or 12½ percent chance of being correct. On the other hand, I knew that each number in my instructions could be followed by only one of two numbers. Consequently, I had a one-in-two or 50 percent chance of being correct. You were more uncertain about what each number would be. Consequently, when you decoded your instructions you had more uncertainty reduced. Your message conveyed more information to you because more numbers could have been used in your message than in mine.

## Bits

The question for the information theorist is to determine precisely how much information a message conveys. We concluded that your instructions encoded from a pool of eight numbers conveyed more information than did my instructions encoded from a pool of two numbers because you were more uncertain initially than I was. Consequently, your instructions reduced more uncertainty than did mine. But how much more information did your instructions convey than mine?

Information theorists measure the amount of information conveyed by a code in terms of "bits." The definition of a bit is *that amount of information necessary to reduce the number of possible signal alternatives by one half.* The task is to determine the fewest number of guesses you and I must make to determine what the next number in our coded instructions will be. Remember that knowing the numbers we have already decoded does not help us guess what the next number in the message will be. We can think of the number of bits of information conveyed by our respective messages as the number of times the pool of signals used to encode our messages must be divided in half to leave the correct signal.

Your instructions are encoded from a pool of eight numbers. Assume these numbers are 0, 1, 2, 3, 4, 5, 6, and 7. I am with you when you receive the message and am curious about how many bits of information your instructions convey. I open your instructions and ask you to guess what the first number is. You guess that it is in the first half of the series (i.e., either 0, 1, 2, or 3). I respond that it is not. It has taken you one guess to reduce the eight initial alternatives by one half. You know now that the first number must be either 4, 5, 6, or 7. You guess that it is either 4 or 5. I respond that it is not. You have now used two guesses and have reduced the remaining four alternatives by half again. You know that the correct number must be either 6 or 7. You guess a third time that the first number in your coded instructions is 7. I respond that it is not. You now know what the first number in your instructions is. But it has taken you three guesses to do so. Stated another way, you had to reduce eight possible alternative signals into halves three times. We now know that, in information theory terms, each number of your coded instructions conveys three bits of information.

When I receive my coded instructions, you decide to play the same game with me. Remember that my instructions are encoded from a pool of two numbers—0 and 1. I guess that the first number of my coded instructions is 0. You respond that it is not. I now know that the first number is 1. I had to guess only once. Since the total number of alternatives was two, it was necessary to divide them in half only once to arrive at the correct alternative. Each number in my coded instructions conveys only one bit of information.

The underlying principle of measuring information in bits is that the number of bits of information conveyed by a signal corresponds to raising the number two to a given power to obtain the number of signals in the coding pool. For example, we raise the base number two to the first power to obtain two, the number of signals in the pool from which my message was encoded. We raise the base number two to the third power to obtain the number of signals in the pool from which your instructions were encoded; two raised to the third power equals eight.

The power to which we raise the base number two corresponds to the number of bits of information conveyed by one signal from a pool containing a total number of signals of two raised to that given power. If your instructions had been encoded from a pool of four numbers, each number in the instructions would have conveyed two bits of information; the base number two raised to the second power equals four, the total number of signals in the coding pool.

Why is the base number we use two? Because a bit is defined as the amount of information required to reduce by half the number of remaining alternatives. We divide the pool of signals by two until the correct signal is identified. The number of times we must divide the total pool of signals by two to arrive at one is the number of bits of information conveyed by each signal in the coding pool. This is where the term "bit" comes from; it is shorthand for "*bi*nary dig*it*."

One of the most important insights of Shannon and Weaver in formulating information theory was that the power function of two is an inverse logarithmic function. Stated another way, the logarithm to the base two of the number two equals one. Written in mathematical language, $\log_2 2 = 1$. Similarly, $\log_2 4 = 2$, $\log_2 8 = 3$, and $\log_2 16 = 4$, and so on. This is simply another way of determining to what power you must raise the number two to arrive at the total number of signals in the coding pool. Shannon and Weaver concluded that for a set of equally probable signals, the logarithm to the base two of the total number of signals in the coding pool is the number of bits of information required to predict which signal is selected.

### Entropy

Entropy is a concept very similar in nature to information. But entropy helps to sharpen our thinking about information by providing us with three different types of information conveyed by messages. In our example of two secret agents receiving coded instructions, you were to assume that all of the numbers in the coding pool were independent of one another and equally probable in occurrence. When that assumption can be made, the amount of information conveyed by each signal in the coding pool equals the logarithm to the base two of the total number of signals in the pool.

But when all the signals in the coding pool are not independent and equally probable, like letters in the English alphabet and words in the English language, computing the amount of information conveyed by a signal is a little more difficult. We now have to take into account that different signals in the coding pool have different probabilities of being selected to encode messages. Without going into Shannon and Weaver's derivation and mathematical proof, we can say that what they do is compute the logarithm to the base two of the probabilities of each of the signals in the pool. Inasmuch as the probabilities of each signal differ, all probabilities are added and then multiplied by the logarithm to the base two of each of those probabilities. The formula for determining the information conveyed by a set of signals of unequal probabilities is:

$H=-\Sigma p_i \log_2 p_i$. That formula reads: information *(H)* equals (=) the sum minus ($\Sigma$) of the probabilities *(p)* of any signal *(i)* multiplied by the logarithm to the base two ($\log_2$) of those probabilities *($p_i$)*. The minus sign is inserted in front of the summation symbol ($\Sigma$) because the logarithm of any number less than one is negative. Probabilities, unless they refer to certainty, in which case we say the probability is one, are numbers less than one. To obtain a positive number for bits of information computed by the formula, the minus sign is inserted to convert the negative logarithm to a positive number.

The term *maximum entropy* refers to the measurement of information in a message encoded from a pool of signals each of which has an equal probability of being used to encode the message. *Absolute entropy* refers to the measurement of information in a message encoded from a pool of signals each of which does not have an equal probability of being used to encode the message. To determine the absolute entropy measure in bits of information we add the probabilities of each signal in the coding pool being used and multiply that figure by the logarithm to the base two of each of the signal probabilities.

Maximum and absolute entropy measures of information are valuable by themselves but they can be combined to tell us the percent of information a message conveys relative to the total amount of information it could convey. This measurement of the relative amount of information is called the *relative entropy* measure of information in bits. Assume we have a pool of signals which we know are not equally probable. For the sake of comparison we can treat each signal in the pool as if it were equally probable and then compare the pool of actual signal probabilities to it. To compute relative entropy we would determine the absolute entropy of the pool of signals and then divide that number by the maximum entropy measure. The resulting number would tell us how much information our pool of signals conveys compared to how much it could convey if the pool were maximally entropic.

## Redundancy

One question the information theorist has about the signals in a coding pool is how predictable the next signal will be given that we know all of the signals that preceded it. This is simply trying to determine how predictable (redundant) rather than how unpredictable (entropic) the signals in a message are.

Let's assume that we have computed the relative entropy for a coding pool of signals to be 80 percent. This means that the signals are 80 percent as unpredictable as they could be if all the signals were equally probable. Redundancy tells us what percentage of the signals in a coding pool are unnecessary if all the signals were to be selected with equal probability. The redundancy of a maximally entropic signal pool is zero because no one signal is selected with any greater or lesser probability than any other signal. To compute the redundancy of a signal pool you subtract the relative entropy measure from unity (or the number one). If our relative entropy for a signal pool is 80 percent, then the redundancy of that pool is 20 percent.

## Channel Capacity

Another question to which Shannon and Weaver addressed themselves was the capacity of a channel for transmitting bits of information. If we know that a channel, whether it be a telegraph wire or a human brain, can process a given number of signals per second, and if we know that the coding pool contains a given number of signals, we can determine how many bits of information per second the channel is capable of transmitting. Let $s$ represent the number of signals per second the channel can transmit. Let $m$ represent the maximum entropy measure of information in bits. Let $a$ represent the absolute entropy measure of information in bits. If all of the signals in the coding pool have an equal probability of being selected, then the capacity ($C$) of the channel, in terms of bits of information it can transmit, is determined by multiplying $m$ by $s$. In short, $C = ms$ when all signals are equally probable. When the signals in the pool are not all equally probable, channel capacity is determined by multiplying the number of signals the channel can transmit per second by the absolute entropy; or $C = as$.

## CHARACTERISTICS OF INFORMATION THEORY

Information theory is an example of what Kaplan (1964) calls the symbolic style of thinking. It is a formal theory because its form is of primary concern; the content is more incidental. A wide range of different phenomena or contents may exemplify the same form or structure. Substantive theories tend to be more specific to a given phenomenon. Granted, Shannon and Weaver started with a rather specific problem to solve. But their explanatory strategy was to identify the formal properties of the problem, use these basic properties as primary statements, then deduce the implications of those statements.

The language of information theory is symbolic, as Kaplan defines that term, and the symbols are those of mathematics. This is an extremely efficient language; many ideas can be condensed into a very short space. Another important property of the language of mathematics is that it facilitates the deduction of secondary statements from primary statements. Stated another way, when mathematical language is used, mathematical transformations can be used to formulate logical deductions. For example, once the power of two was seen to underlie the encoding-decoding process, the mathematical function of logarithms was made available as well as all the logarithmic transformations. These transformations allowed the theorems of absolute and relative entropy to be deduced.

The metaphor underlying information theory is mechanistic. We are asked to think of machines or devices used to transmit signals from one point to another. How applicable this theory of the syntactic dimension of communication is to the semantic and pragmatic dimensions is not clear. Some attempts have been made but other researchers are critical of such attempted applications. At base, one objection is on aesthetic grounds; some find it repugnant to conceive of human communication in mechanistic terms. Other objections focus on methodological grounds; how can semantic meaning be quantified in terms similar to syntactic information? However these issues resolve themselves, it must be admitted that for its explanatory purposes, information theory is effective.

It should be noted that information theory, like most formal theories when compared to substantive theories, is the most parsimonious theory we have discussed. From five primary statements, twenty-three theorems have been deduced. The ratio of primary to secondary statements is most impressive.

*And how will you investigate, Socrates, that of which you know nothing at all? Where can you find a starting-point in the region of the unknown? And even if you happen to come full upon what you want, how will you ever know that this is the thing which you did not know?*

**PLATO** *Meno*

# Theory as Explanation

8

## INTRODUCTION

Having considered four types of theories and representative examples of each in previous chapters, this chapter moves on to discuss how theories are used to explain what was previously unexplainable. Specifically, concatenated and hierarchical forms of theory are presented as a backdrop against which four different explanatory activities are highlighted. These explanatory activities assist in illustrating the direction of theoretical development in areas of intellectual concern. Finally, six functions of theory are treated and the chapter concludes by dislodging any misconception that the growth and function of theory is an orderly and accumulative process.

## CONCATENATED AND HIERARCHICAL THEORIES

By way of review and also as a basis of discussion in this chapter, Figure 3 is presented to illustrate the types of statements needed to construct Type I, II, III (which are substantive) and IV (which is formal) Theories and the order of those statements in each Theory Type.

Of these four types of theories, Kaplan (1964) would call the Type III and IV Theories hierarchical and Types I and II concatenated (p.298). A hierarchical formal theory is "one whose component laws are presented as deductions from a small set of basic principles" (Kaplan, 1964, p.298). A hierarchical substantive theory consists of warranted assertions derived from propositions about the empirical world. The hierarchy is a derivative or deductive pyramid.

Type I and II Theories, on the other hand, are similar to what Kaplan calls concatenated theories. They are theories whose component statements enter into a network of relations so as to constitute an identifiable configuration or pattern (Kaplan, 1964, p.298). A concatenated theory consists of postulates and axioms which, taken together, form a pattern that explains a particular phenomenon. Duncan's (1968) theory of social order is a good example. Although hypotheses can be derived from theorems, secondary statements are inferred. It is the inferential network of primary and

Theory                    Necessary Steps of Theory Construction

| | | | | | | | | | | |
|---|---|---|---|---|---|---|---|---|---|---|
| Type I | (Assume) | Axioms | (Add) | Postulates | (Infer) | Theorems | (Derive) | Hypotheses | | |
| Type II | (Assume) | Postulates | (Infer) | Theorems | (Derive) | Hypotheses | | | | |
| Type III | (Assume) | Propositions | (Derive) | Hypotheses | | | | | | |
| Type IV | (Assume) | Primary Statements | (Deduce) | Theorems | | | | | | |

**Fig. 3.** The types of theoretical statements, their order, and their relation to each other in constructing the four Theory Types discussed.

secondary statements which, taken together, constitute an explanation. The 36 theoretical statements of Duncan's theory form a network more than a pyramidal or hierarchical explanation.

In a hierarchical theory, the statements derived or deduced from the primary set test the explanation. This is true in ego-involvement theory, for example. In a concatenated theory, the test is more indirect, via statements inferred from the network of semantically and syntactically valid statements.

In the social sciences it is somewhat premature to talk of theory construction in the same ways as do the natural sciences. Whereas many natural sciences build formally deductive theories comprised of universal or near-universal laws, few of the social sciences are prepared to argue they have any universally supported claims. Nevertheless, some social science theories are more general than others and, as such, are more parsimonious.

As a rule, a hierarchical substantive theory (i.e., a Type III Theory such as ego-involvement theory) is more general and more parsimonious than a concatenated substantive theory (i.e., Type I and II Theories such as Burke's or Duncan's). The former contain fewer theoretical statements (minimally one proposition from which at least one hypothesis can be derived) and are more derivative in nature than are concatenated theories. Concatenated theories, because the primary statements are semantically or syntactically rather than empirically valid, of necessity are more inferential than deductive or derivative in form.

## Triangulation

Stated another way, inasmuch as many concepts in each primary statement of Type I and II Theories are not observable, such theories must gain their explanatory strength from a triangulation process. One statement contains some operationally defined concepts that none of the other statements contains. Thus, by adding increasingly more statements to the network, eventually most of the essential concepts become empirical. The strengths and weaknesses of the concatenated (partially overlapping) statements complement each other and provide a sufficiently strong network from which theorems can be inferred. Figure 4 distinguishes the four Theory Types in terms of their content scope, structural form, and validity claim.

| Theory type | Content scope | | Structural form | | | Validity claim | | | |
|---|---|---|---|---|---|---|---|---|---|
| | General | Universal | Inferential | Derivative | Deductive | Syntactical | Semantical | Empirical | Tautological |
| I (Concatenated) | X | | X | | | X | | | |
| II (Concatenated) | X | | X | | | | X | | |
| III (Hierarchical) | X | | | X | | | | X | |
| IV (Hierarchical) | | X | | | X | | | | X |

Fig. 4.  The four Theory Types defined in terms of their content scope, structural form, and validity claims. Types I, II, and III are substantive theories and Type IV is formal. The Xs in the cells refer to an instance of the category terms.

## THE ACTIVITY OF EXPLANATION

The traditionally stated goals of science are to *predict, control,* and *explain.* Of the three, however, explanation is the most fundamental. It is possible to predict without either controlling or explaining the events predicted. An example of such a case is astronomy, where the orbits of planets and trajectories of comets could be predicted before they could be explained. And, of course, the probability of these phenomena being controlled is very small (Handy, 1964, pp.14, 15). In the social sciences, shaping or modeling behavior in animals and humans can be predicted and, to some extent, controlled (Bandura, 1969). But there remains significant disagreement over which theory constitutes the most satisfactory explanation of this modeling phenomenon.

### "Scientific" Explanation

The term "explanation," however, refers to several different activities. Taylor (1970) discusses four activities to which the term most frequently refers and Monge's (1973) summary of Taylor's discussion is most helpful at this point. The most rigorous explanation is formal (a Type IV Theory). Taylor calls a formal theory a "scientific explanation." " 'Scientific explanation' ... consists of a universal generalization that is assumed to be true, a particular set of circumstances, and a conclusion which asserts that an event had to occur because it was deducible from the logic of the propositions of the theory" (Monge, 1973, p.6).

The key terms here are "universal" and "deducible." In this sense of the term, for a theory to be a "scientific explanation" it must be universal in applicability and, following the canons of logic, other universally applicable statements must be deduced from the primary statements. If this use of "explanation" is adhered to, few social science theories can be said to explain. One reason is because sufficient data do not yet exist to support many universal statements. Most of the existing data are relative to both culture and population, consequently these theories are substantive rather than formal.

Taylor (1970) would say information theory qualifies as a "scientific explanation." The theory is causal; it accounts for *why* different coding pools are more efficient than others; *why* channels have certain transmission capacities; and *why* noise influences transmission efficiency. Information theory has generated a modest amount of empirical work in the social sciences. Its theorems are tautologically valid but the extent of their empirical validity remains to be determined.

## "What" Explanation

The second form of explanation is less demanding but also less satisfying. " 'What-explanations' are attempts to specify what a phenomenon is. It is an explanation in that it removes uncertainty about the object by classifying and categorizing it with other phenomena; but it does not explain *why* the phenomenon is classified the way it is" (Monge, 1973, p.6).

This activity is very similar to description except instead of the parts of an event being classified into concepts, the entire event is classified. Such an activity is somewhat more conjectural than simply listing facts, although not as abstract and conceptual as the activity of ordering statements to construct a substantive theory.

Taylor (1970) would label Duncan's theory as a "what explanation." Clearly, Duncan is calling for an explanation of how social integration is achieved through communication. But his theory does not provide the answer in terms of a "causal" or "why" or "scientific explanation." His theory tells us *what* to observe but not why it is important to observe it.

## "Mental-concept" Explanation

Taylor (1970) says such explanations are the result of a third activity. This form of explanation is advanced primarily by scientists engaged in correlational research. Certain concepts are selected as variables (a variable usually is what an operationally defined concept is called) to assess their interrelationships. When relationships are found, the phenomenon is said to be explained by the cluster of variables. "To use one of these concepts [motive, intention, belief, ability, knowledge, and disposition] to explain a person's action is to describe that action as a part of a pattern of behavior. . . . Thus, mental-concept explanations are what-explanations. They do not attempt to relate two things in such a way that one could be predicted from the other" (Monge, 1973, p.7).

Mental-concept explanations usually are in the form of a concatenous theory (i.e., a Type I or II Theory) because the concepts, like the statements in which they are embedded, explain by virtue of their interrelationships rather than by virtue of the statements that can be derived directly from them.

Taylor (1970) would call ego-involvement theory an example of a "mental-concept explanation" even though the objective of the theory is to predict attitudes and their changes. The reason is that the central concept is a mental or internal variable that is used to explain behavior. As the number of supported hypotheses derived from the theorems increases, the theory will grow in its predictive capacity and qualify as a "scientific explanation" (Taylor, 1970).

### "Reason-giving" Explanation

Monge (1973) says, " 'Reason-giving explanations' are similar to 'mental-concept' explanations; they account for why certain phenomena occur by showing why a person thought that a particular action or belief was right, correct, true, or a good thing to do. . . . Thus, reason-giving explanations allow us to *assess* a person's behavior in terms of the evaluative views he holds preceding his action, and nothing more" (pp.7, 8). This explanatory activity also results in concatenated rather than hierarchical theory.

Burke's theory of motives is what Taylor (1970) calls a "reason-giving explanation." Insofar as the central concept of the theory is usually an after-the-fact attribution to behavior, it is used to invest behaviors with meaning or a *raison d'être*. It is important to underline the idea that Burke is interested in the motives both others and the actors involved attribute to behaviors. Burke does not claim to, nor does he want to, find the reasons or motivations or causes of human behavior in the logical senses of those terms.

Each of these forms of explanation differs in terms of the scope of the statements; i.e., whether they are universal or relative, and the relationship among the statements; i.e., whether some are derived from others or all are loosely interrelated.

## FORMS OF EXPLANATION

For a theory to provide what Taylor (1970) calls a "scientific explanation," it is necessary to have universal generalizations that cover all instances of a phenomenon. For universal statements to be made, a field must be researched sufficiently to provide a rich variety of supported hypotheses that function as warranted assertions.

These assertions then must be tested further until they can be treated as propositions, postulates, or axioms. If the statements derived from these primary statements add further support, propositions can be treated as laws. These laws then are used as primary universal statements from which other universally true statements can be deduced.

In ascending order of generality, a *fact* is a single case of a concept considered true in that one instance. A *hypothesis* is an assertion of relationship between two or more facts in a small and finite number of cases. Depending upon the number of observable concepts in them, supported hypotheses are considered to be true in an indefinitely large yet finite number of cases. *Propositions, postulates,* and *axioms* that are further supported are considered to be true of a universal and infinite number of cases. Formal theories are constructed only after a relatively large number of substantive theories have been tested.

## Direction of Theory Development

The typical direction of theoretical development in a new science is from concatenated-substantive theories to hierarchical-substantive theories, to hierarchical-formal theories. Most of the social science theories explain not by specifying logical causes of the phenomenon but rather by identifying empirical relations of the phenomenon. Causal, or what Taylor (1970) calls "scientific," explanations are relatively late in developing because the criteria for their construction are so stringent. Consequently, many social science theories are concatenated "what," "mental-concept," and "reason-giving" explanations. These theories are more relational or mutually causal rather than deductive or directly causal in form.

## Extension and Intension

Knowledge in any science grows in one or a combination of two ways; either by *extension* or *intension* (Kaplan, 1964, pp.304–306). With extensional growth, a small region of the terrain is explained fully and then used to explain other parts of the region. Kaplan says this is much like an "erector set" conception of knowledge growth; small pieces are added together until larger regions are understood (p.305). Hierarchical theories develop knowledge extensionally; given a small set of initial statements, a wide range of implications is derived thus broadening the knowledge base. Ego-involvement and information theory are good examples of theories that develop the knowledge base extensionally.

Intensional growth of knowledge is making more satisfactory the explanation of a large area. The effect is a gradual focusing-in on more specific knowledge claims (Kaplan, 1964, p.305). Concatenated theories are associated usually with the intensional growth of knowledge. As such, Burke and Duncan's theories are examples of theories leading to the intensional growth of knowledge and understanding. Extensional growth increases the scope as well as the detail of knowledge; intensional growth decreases the scope but increases the detail of knowledge.

In a new science, such as speech communication, concatenated-substantive (Type I and II) theories are the first to develop as knowledge is growing intensionally. Scientists are struggling to define the most fruitful regions for investigation. Concatenated-substantive theories help the scientist focus-in on increasingly more relevant phenomena. As the science matures, concatenated-substantive theories continue to be constructed as new terrain is explored. But hierarchical-substantive (Type III) theories are constructed and facilitate the extensional growth of knowledge. Knowledge of specific phenomena is added together thus broadening the range of detailed understanding. Finally, in the most abstract and general disciplines (e.g., logic, mathematics), hierarchical-formal theories (Type IV) are constructed as knowledge grows almost exclusively by extension.

## FUNCTIONS OF THEORY

Barnlund (1968, pp.18–21) mentions six advantages of what are referred to here as hierarchical-formal theories. These advantages accrue to theories in proportion to their degree of universality of content and formality of form. Stated another way, the more a theory tends to be cast in literary or academic language, the more likely it is to be general in scope, concatenated in form, and semantically or syntactically valid. Such theories are least likely to enjoy the functions about to be discussed. On the other hand, the more formal the language of the theory, the more likely it is to be universal in context, hierarchical in form and empirically or tautologically valid.

## Clarification

The first function of theory is to *add clarity* to the concepts playing a role in that theory. The more deductive—as opposed to derivative or relational—the form of the theory, the easier it is to identify inconsistencies, ambiguities, and omissions in it. The advantage of deductive form is that statements deduced from a primary set are implicit in the primary set and deduction makes them explicit. Once explicated, inconsistencies and omissions in the primary set of propositions, postulates, and axioms are made more apparent.

When a theory is derivative in form, it is more difficult to identify source of the inconsistency or ambiguity. Inasmuch as hypotheses are derived by implication rather than deduced by logic, it is more difficult to identify the troublesome concepts and clarify them. The clarifying function is practically absent in a concatenated theory because its form is merely relational. When confusion exists, the usual procedure is to add more statements to the existing network, or rephrase some of the statements.

## Detection

The second function of theory is to *detect hidden assumptions*. The more a theory permits logical deductions, the less likely it is that assumptions will remain unstated on the tacit level. For example, in many social science theories it is not always made clear that statements are culture and sometimes population specific (Toulmin, 1969). The more deductive the form, the more the assumptions have to be made specific for logically valid deductions to be made.

## Verification

Capitalizing on *indirect verification* is the third function of theory. As the number of hypothetical statements deduced or derived and supported increases, the more likely it becomes that support for one theoretical statement directly or indirectly supports other statements of the same or related theories. For example, some of the warranted assertions of ego-involvement theory indirectly supports some of the warranted assertions of persuasibility theory. If some persons are more persuasible than others, it is, at least in part, a function of their degree of involvement in the issue.

### Relation

Specifying the *range of relevance* is a fourth function. The more deductive the form of a theory, the easier it is to determine how new information affects it. The connection between data, hypotheses, and propositions or theorems is more apparent the more deductive the theory.

In a relational theory, such as Duncan's (1968) theory of social order, it is difficult to determine how evidence supporting or falsifying the "axiomatic propositions" can be related to the "theoretical propositions." The connection between these two sets of statements which defines the range of the theory is impossible to ascertain as they now stand. If Duncan's theory were more deductive in form and more empirically valid, that difficulty would be minimized.

### Identification

The more deductive in form, the more a theory is capable of *identifying equivalent properties* in other theories. This function is important in the scientific activity of model-building, as we shall see later. As the range of relevance of a theory increases, so does the probability that other theories exist which explain some or all of the same or similar phenomena.

In doing science, integrating similar properties of different theories increases the explanatory potential of a theory. This identification process is easier to accomplish, and therefore more likely to occur, if hypotheses stand in a logical relation to the propositions from which they were derived or deduced.

### Suggestion

The last, and in many ways the most important, function of theory is its *heuristic capacity*. The more deductive in form and empirical in validity, the more likely a theory is to generate new hypotheses. Suggestive theories are referred to frequently as "rich" or "heuristic" because they inspire so much scientific investigation. Theories of attitude change have generated much research primarily because the primary set of statements and the subsequent warranted assertions, although not universal in content and deductive in form, suggest many related and testable hypotheses. For a theory to gain any degree of scientific stature, it must be heuristic because only through extensive testing can it be supported or falsified.

## PARADIGMATIC SHIFTS

From the discussion of forms of explanation and functions of theory, you should not conclude that scientific inquiry results in a steady accumulation of knowledge eventuating in ultimate and complete understanding. Any science, and its subspecialities, rests on a set of assumptions about what legitimate puzzles exist to be solved and what form satisfactory solutions should take.

Kuhn (1970) contends that "normal science" can be thought of as this kind of puzzle-solving activity. During normal puzzle-solving activity, when theories are tested, falsified, and extended, certain rules are adhered to concerning appropriate questions to ask and methods to use. The underlying assumptions of a scientific community are seldom articulated because everyone assumes them predominantly on a tacit level (Polanyi, 1958). These underlying and tacitly held assumptions that dictate abstract rules for doing science Kuhn calls *paradigms* (pp.43–51).

Regarding the nature of paradigms, Kuhn says that scientists can "agree in their *identification* of a paradigm without agreeing on, or even attempting to produce, a full *interpretation* or *rationalization* of it. Lack of a standard interpretation or of an agreed reduction to rules will not prevent a paradigm from guiding research. . . . Indeed, the existence of a paradigm need not even imply that any full set of rules exists." (p.44)

What Kuhn is saying, in brief, is that when all is going well in a particular science, no one is very concerned about questioning why they are asking the questions they are and using the methods they do. It is assumed that the basic approach to, or paradigm for, the science is appropriate. Scientists are concerned with adding knowledge extensionally by solving more parts of the puzzle.

### Intellectual Conflict

But these basic assumptions that characterize the paradigm do not remain unquestioned indefinitely. Kuhn says, "Normal science can proceed without rules only so long as the relevant scientific community accepts without question the particular problem-solutions already achieved. Rules should therefore become important and the characteristic unconcern about them should vanish whenever paradigms or models are felt to be insecure." (p.47)

This insecurity usually is the result of a series of unexpected answers to questions; answers that continue to falsify or cast doubt on a broad range of specific theories resting on those tacit, paradigmatic assumptions. In physics, for example, phenomena increasingly were found not to fit into or support theories based on the Newtonian paradigm. The result was the quantum mechanics paradigm as a replacement. There was much debate and disagreement regarding the nature of physics that accompanied this shift in paradigms. But once the new paradigm is accepted, theories based on the previous paradigm are treated as obsolete and the process of knowledge acquisition, both intensionally and extensionally, begins anew.

Kuhn says of the dissention surrounding paradigm shifts, "debates like these do not vanish once and for all with the appearance of a paradigm. Though almost nonexistent during periods of normal science, they recur regularly just before and during scientific revolutions, the periods when paradigms are first under attack and then subject to change." (p.48)

*... the domain of truth has no fixed boundaries within it. In the one world of ideas there are no barriers to trade or to travel. Each discipline may take from others techniques, concepts, laws, data, models, theories, or explanations—in short, whatever it finds useful for its own inquiries.*

**ABRAHAM KAPLAN**   *The Conduct of Inquiry*

**9**

# Model Building

## INTRODUCTION

What is a model? Is a model different from a theory and, if so, in what respects? Why do social scientists build models? What are the functions of models in the doing of social science?

Within the social science community there is anything but widespread agreement about the answers to these questions. In fact, answers are as plentiful as are the people concerned with the questions. Acknowledging this confusing state of affairs, however, is not to accept and condone it. This chapter offers one set of answers to these questions. The answers are grounded, to a large extent, in the philosophies of social science articulated by Max Black (1962), Robert Brown (1963), Abraham Kaplan (1964), May Brodbeck (1968), Robert Dubin (1969),and Karl Pearson (1969). Not all social scientists agree with the answers to be provided and the perspectives from which they emerge. The answers to be advocated in this chapter, however, hold greater promise than some others for the development of communication as a sophisticated social science.

There are many types of models, some of which will not be examined. For example, the term when used to refer to a norm or value (e.g., speaking of someone exhibiting model behavior) or style (e.g., speaking of fall models of clothing or new car models) is of little interest. Models that further theory development in the doing of social science are the focus of this chapter. Toward this end, this chapter considers some of the differences between theories and models, the process by which models are constructed, several criteria for evaluating models, generally recognized functions of models, and finally some generally held misconceptions of models.

## DEFINITION OF A MODEL

Perhaps the simplest definition of a model is that it is an analogue; a model is a relatively well-developed analogy. Given two objects or processes which are dissimilar in many respects, one is an analogue of the other to the extent that the physical or logical structure of one *re-presents* the physical or logical structure of the other. It is the identification of the significant structural and/or functional similarities, ones which generate new insights and questions, that is the challenge in the art of model building.

The world abounds with pedestrian analogues. It is, from Bronowski's (1965) perspective, the identification of unity in apparent disunity, the formulation of stubbornly implicit analogies, that leads to significant advances in the understanding of behavior.

## DIFFERENCES BETWEEN MODELS AND THEORIES

The most fundamental difference between a theory and a model is that the former is an *explanation* whereas the latter is a *representation*. A theory is an explanation insofar as it accounts for the causal or correlative relations among its component concepts. Recall that theoretical statements consist of substantive and logical terms. It is the logical terms that explain the substantive terms (i.e., concepts) and it is the relations among the theoretical statements that constitutes the explanation of the object phenomenon.

A model, on the other hand, *re-presents* salient structural and/ or functional features, properties, or characteristics of another object or process. A model is not an explanation; it is only the structure and/or function of a second object or process. A model is the result of taking the structure or function of the one object or process and using that as a model for the second. When the substance, either physical or conceptual, of the second object or process has been projected onto the first, a model has been constructed. The structure or function of the first object or process is said to model the second.

For example, the following diagram is a network structure. It can be used to represent such things as a methane molecule, individuals in a small group, or branch offices of a business conglomerate. To the extent that this structure represents the structure of a

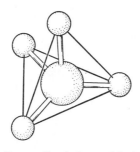

**Fig. 5** (From John R. Raser. *Simulation and Society: An Explanation of Scientific Gaming.* Boston: Allyn and Bacon, 1969, p. 7. Reprinted by permission.)

molecule, a small group, and a business conglomerate, it can be used to model those objects.

The structure of the network by itself, however, is not a model because what it re-presents is not yet specified. When the object or process to be represented by it is "mapped" onto it, the structure functions as a model. But even after the mapping is completed (i.e., the elements of the model are given specific referents), the model is not a theory. The relations among the elements are not yet explained; they are re-presented only via the structure of a network.

## THE MAPPING PROCESS

### Analogue

Mapping is a term which refers to the systematic application of substance (i.e., concepts) to structure (i.e., logical and/or physical relations). Three important terms must be defined to explicate fully the mapping process—analogue, structure, and model. An *analogue* is a relatively well-developed theory, frequently a theory from a seemingly unrelated discipline or about unrelated substance, which is used to assist in the development of a theory presently less developed than the analogue.

Consider, for example, the state of scientists' ability to explain the "spread" of new information and innovations in a community or culture. Prior to the work of Katz (1957, 1961), Katz and Lazarsfeld (1955), Rogers (1962), and Rogers and Shoemaker (1971) on the diffusion of innovation and the work of some rural sociologists, social science theories of this process were not very well developed. At some point, the better developed theories of epidemiology, which explained the "spread" of diseases, were used as analogues; some similarity in the dynamics of the two "spread" phenomena was suspected. Epidemiological theories, replete with medical concepts, were the analogues for developing more sophisticated explanations of "spread" and "diffusion" phenomena in the social sciences.

### Structure

For an analogue to assist in the development of a theory, the substance (i.e., conceptual material) of the analogue must be stripped away leaving only its *structure*. A theory, as discussed in Chapter 3, can be thought of in terms of its structure and substance. Theories vary along a continuum in terms of their structure/substance ratio. Type I Theories are concerned primarily with substance and only secondarily with the structure of the substance. At the other extreme, Type IV Theories are concerned primarily with structure and only secondarily with substance. It is for this reason that more completely developed theories are used as analogues for less developed theories; the structure of the more developed theory is more manifest and readily identifiable.

It is easier to disentangle substance from structure in a Type III or IV Theory than in Type I or II Theory; less effort need be expended stripping away the substance of the more fully developed theory to reveal its structure. Stripping away the substance of a theory transforms that theory, when used as an analogue, into a structure. When medical substance is removed from a theory of epidemiology, its logical structure is all that remains.

## Model

The mapping process involves projecting the substance of the less developed theory onto the structure. The result of this procedure is a *model*. When informational concepts are mapped onto the structure of the epidemiological theory, a model of the diffusion of innovation and information has been created. The model re-presents innovation and information concepts via the structure of an epidemiological theory used as an analogue.

In short, a model is the structure of an analogue onto which different substance has been mapped. If the same derivations or deductions hold for the new substance as did for the stripped away substance, the new substance is said to be explained by the old structure, now functioning as a model. When the explanation is satisfactorily complete, the model ceases to function as a model and is now thought of as a theory; one which is partially isomorphic to the original theory.

## Isomorphism

The more developed theory, the one whose logical structure functions as a model, and the less developed theory, the one whose substance is modeled by that logical structure, are said to be isomorphic to the extent that the derivations and deductions holding for the more developed theory also hold for the less developed theory. By using the more fully developed structure as the model for the more ill-defined theory, the development of the latter is facilitated and its explanatory potential is enhanced.

The range of theories whose logical structures can be used as models of and for less developed theories is practically limitless. A model-builder in the communication discipline is by no means restricted to that discipline in searching for theories to function as analogues. In fact, some of the most exciting advances in the social sciences have resulted from using theories from seemingly dissimilar disciplines as analogues.

### Mathematical Analogues

The preceding explanation holds when the structure of a Type II Theory functions as a model for a Type I Theory, a Type III Theory functions as a model for a Type II or Type I Theory, or a Type IV Theory provides the structure for a Type III, II, or I Theory. But when a pure mathematical language is sought expressly to provide the structure, we say the mathematical expression is a model *of* a theory. No content need be stripped away from the mathematical "analogue" (see Brodbeck, 1968, pp.587–588). It is assumed that the object or process being mapped onto the mathematical expression can be manipulated like the mathematical expression.

In short, when empirical or substantive theories are used as analogues *for* other theories, the implications or derivations are empirically or substantively based. When mathematical expressions are used as analogues *of* other theories, the deductions are formally or logically based. Formal theories are more general than substantive theories.

## CRITERIA FOR EVALUATING MODELS

### Heuristics

Although model-builders have some license concerning which conceptual materials can be mapped onto which structures, they must satisfy certain criteria for the structure to function as a model. The most important criterion is that sufficient information about the structural and/or functional properties of the analogue be available to produce insightful questions and/or hypotheses. The purpose of building a model is to use an analogue about whose structure something is known and map onto that structure conceptual material about whose structure and/or function less is known. In short, the model must be heuristic.

There must be sufficient information about the structural properties of the theory serving as the analogue so that similar properties in the structure and/or function of the object being modeled can be tested. If no more is known about the structure of a theory functioning as the analogue than about the material being modeled, mapping the latter onto the former is simply an exercise in futility; it serves no heuristic purpose.

### Isomorphism

The second criterion a model-builder must satisfy is that there be at least a partial isomorphism between the analogue and the theoretical material to be modeled. Isomorphism, you recall, is a term referring to the degree of similarity in the structure and/or function of the two objects or processes. If two objects are completely isomorphic they are said to be identical and, therefore, the same object. Neither is a model for the other; they are identical. Few objects or processes in the social sciences, however, are thought to be completely isomorphic.

It is quite possible to have extensive information about the structural properties of the analogue and not to have examined the structure of the material to be mapped onto it. The result is a poor fit of the object or process being modeled and the structure of the analogue. One can expect inappropriate questions and hypotheses at best, and nonsense questions and hypotheses at worst, from such a mismatch.

### Correspondence

The third criterion is that the model-builder must specify the *rules of correspondence* between the structure and its mapped material. In a sense, this criterion demands that the model-builder specify the procedures of his mapping process. Recognizing and adhering to this criterion are important for two reasons: first, others are enabled to check on the adequacy of the mapping procedure; and second, the model can be interpreted and made clear.

Specifying the rules of correspondence in model building is similar in purpose and function to operationally defining concepts in theory construction. If one is to test the adequacy of an explanation (i.e., theory) or the utility of a representation (i.e., model), the procedures leading up to its present form must allow for independent verification.

## FUNCTIONS OF MODELS

The most important purpose of model building is to assist in the development of more precise and more general theories. It is only logical, then, to develop as precise and as general models of or for theory building as possible. It is the goal of the social sciences to develop Type III and IV Theories of human behavior relying, as much as possible, on mathematical models for help in the process.

This is not to say that all theories of human behavior, at the present time, can be constructed in Type III or IV form; it is to say that is the goal toward which most of the social sciences are striving. It is essential to build models that are neither too simplistic nor too advanced for the theory being developed. The fit between model and theory must be maximally heuristic for the model building effort to be worthwhile. For example, positing a mathematical model for communication aesthetics theory may not be maximally heuristic *at this time;* not because mapping the substantive material of aesthetics to a mathematical structure is not possible *eventually,* but because a conceptual model may be of more assistance *at this time* for developing the theory. Specifically, models can assist in the development of theories in several functional ways; we will discuss the three most important functions.

### Descriptive Function

A model can be constructed to describe a particular form of behavior of which either no theory exists or the theory is grossly inadequate. The purpose of the model in this case is to describe the behavior of interest with more precision and specificity by using a model to represent the underlying structure of the behavior. Once a more adequate description is accomplished, a more comprehensive theory of the phenomenon can be constructed.

One example of modeling for descriptive purposes in communication research is the work of Hawes and Foley (1973) in dyadic interviewing. Traditionally the interview has been investigated as the predictive instrument. Much interest was expressed in how well job success, success in the armed forces, success in school, and success in psychiatric treatment could be predicted from a person's behavior in an interview. The general conclusion from most of this research is that the interview is not an impressive predictive instrument. Little attention, however, was paid to the interviewing process itself. What communicative patterns of behavior did the interviewer and interviewee enact during the interview itself that might account for the interview's inability to be used as a reliable predictor of outcome conditions?

The purpose of the Hawes and Foley research was to describe more precisely the communicative behavior defining the initial medical interview. The descriptive function of modeling is the most conservative function; its range of generalizability (i.e., external validity) is narrow and its assumptions are restrictively simplistic. In keeping with the conservative limits on their task, Hawes and Foley used a finite-state discrete-time Markov chain as an analogue for the initial medical interview process. A finite-state discrete-time Markov chain is a particular type of stochastic theory about systems that occupy (or are defined on) a specified number of conditions (or states) and time is thought of as being unitized (or discrete) rather than flowing (or continuous). Systems with finite states operating in discrete time are simpler and easier to analyze than are systems with an infinite number of states defined in continuous time.

The structure of this Markov chain theory was used to model the initial medical interview. Mapping the conceptual material of the interview onto the Markov chain structure resulted in a model which represented the interview as a finite-state discrete-time system. The interviewer and interviewee become the components of the system; their verbal behavior became the elements interconnecting the components in discrete time; and the verbal behavior also defined the twelve states the system occupied at any one point in time.

The simplifying assumptions that had to be made to test the representational value of the model were that: 1) the source of the behavior (i.e., the interviewer and interviewee) was *ergodic* (i.e., the interview could move from any state to any other state of the system); and, 2) any behavior enacted was determined only by the behavior immediately preceding it (i.e., any behavior had no long-range or long-term impact on future behavior).

These two assumptions may seem so restrictive to you that you question the importance or relevance of such a modeling effort. The purpose of descriptive modeling, however, is to begin with the most simplistic representation. If that proves inadequate and its assumptions cannot be met, modifications are made. As it turned out in the Hawes and Foley research, the structure of the finite-state discrete-time Markov chain was a fairly representational description of the initial medical interview. The source was, for all practical purposes, ergodic but some states were better predictors of the next state to be occupied than were others.

These conclusions apply only to the specific interviews modeled. The next step is to make those mathematical operations permitted by Markov chain theory to test the predictive power of the model. If permissible mathematical operations do predict actual behavior, concrete steps have been taken in the development of a more sophisticated theory of interviewing.

## Explicative Function

A second function of model-building is to explicate more fully one important but poorly developed concept in an existing theory. Here the purpose of modeling is not to describe some behavior and thereby make that phenomenon more amenable to theoretical explanation; rather, it is to define more rigorously a concept central to relatively well-developed theory thereby rendering that theory more testable.

Berger *et al.* (1962) provide an example of an explicative model; Cartwright and Harary's (1956) construction of a graph model of the concept of balance in Heider's (1944, 1946, 1958) theory of interpersonal relations. Heider's theory posited a balance between a person's "attitudes" and "causal units." Heider defined attitudes as sentiments such as hating, loving, respecting, and loathing. Causal units were defined as relations between a person and another object or event when it could be assumed that the person caused the event or object. "Peter gave a speech" is a causal unit because the person is assumed to be the cause of the event. Balance was defined as a condition in which two people had similar attitudes about both parts of the causal unit. For example, "Fred likes Peter; Peter gave a speech, Fred likes the speech" is a balanced condition.

Heider assumed that people tried to keep their interpersonal relationships in a balanced condition. He concluded, after some preliminary research, that "a balanced state is one in which there are only positive or one positive and two negative relations between entities related by cognitive and affective ties" (Berger *et al.*, 1962, p.103).

Cartwright and Harary (1956) constructed a model, not of Heider's complete theory but of the key concept of balance. The purpose of the model was to explicate that one concept in fuller detail. Cartwright and Harary recognized the similarity between graph theory and field theory, and between field theory and the concept of balance. Consequently, graph theory became the analogue for the concept of balance.

Graph theory is concerned with *points, lines* connecting points, and the *graph* resulting when some or all of the points are connected by lines. There are five fundamental types of graphs. 1) The *Simple Linear* graph has a set of points connected by symmetric and unsigned lines. 2) *Signed* graphs have points connected by symmetric signed lines (the sign, either + or –, indicates a positive or negative relation between the points connected by the lines). 3) *Directed* graphs are points connected by asymmetric, unsigned lines. 4) *Type T* graphs have two lines connecting each point. In short, each point of the graph is connected to two points, rather than just to one. 5) *Signed-Directed* graphs have points connected by lines that are both signed and directional.

Although Maruyama did not fully exploit the theory of graphs in his representation of urban population dynamics (see Figure 8), his illustration is a graph. Specifically, it is a signed-directed graph because the lines indicate both the direction of influence of the concepts represented by the points and whether that influence is direct (+) or inverse (–).

The rules of correspondence for transforming the graph theory analogue into a model of the concept of balance were that the concepts of point, line, and graph were stripped away and replaced with the concepts of entity, relation, and system. The result of this mapping procedure was an explicative model. The structures of the five types of graphs now represent, or model, five types of relationships for which balanced and unbalanced conditions could be defined and tested for.

Berger *et al.* say of this particular explicative model, "This [the model] permitted them [Cartwright and Harary] to clarify ambiguities in the concept of balance, to extend the application of the concept to systems involving more entities than Heider originally dealt with, and to refine the concept of balance—particularly through the idea of degrees of balance" (p.103).

## Simulative Function

Not all models serve a simulative function, just as not all models serve a descriptive or explicative function. Whether one wants to build a model to describe a phenomenon, explicate a concept, or simulate a process depends upon what immediate steps need to be taken to further develop the theory with which one is concerned. Whereas models that describe and explicate usually represent structural relations among concepts of a theory, models that simulate represent functional or process relations among concepts.

To appreciate the simulative function of models, the distinction between structure and process must be scrutinized more closely. Miller (1965) describes this difference in the following way.

> The *structure* of a system is the arrangement of its subsystems and components in three-dimensional space at a given moment of time. . . . This may remain relatively fixed over a long period or it may change from moment to moment, depending upon the characteristics of the process in the system. This process halted at any given moment—as when motion is frozen by a high-speed camera—reveals the three-dimensional spatial arrangement of the system's components as of that instant. When anatomists study structure, they use dead, often fixed, material in which no further activity can be expected to occur. Similarly historians study the relationships among units of a society at a given period. These are studies of structure.

> All change over time of matter-energy or information in a system is *process*. If the equation describing a process is the

same no matter whether the temporal variable is positive or negative, it is a *reversible* process; otherwise it is *irreversible*. Process includes the on-going *function* of a system, reversible actions succeeding each other from moment to moment. . . . Process also includes history, less readily reversed changes like mutations, birth, growth, development, aging and death; changes which commonly follow trauma or disease; and the changes resulting from learning which is not later forgotten. Historical processes alter both the structure and the function of the system. (p.209)

As we described a theory in Chapter 3 it is a system of component statements and the relations connecting those statements resulting in an explanation. Models that represent these relations at any point in time; i.e., models that represent the static relations among components of a system, are models of structure. On the other hand, models that represent changes in the components of a system, as well as the relations among components over time, are dynamic or models of function (process). Crow (1967) makes the distinction between structure and function as follows.

As a model is a specific form of theory, so a simulation is a specific variety of model, distinguished by the fact that a simulation is a dynamic or operating model; therefore changes over time in the model correspond to changes over time in the system being modeled. In a model, the structural relationships are isomorphic with that being modeled; in a simulation, in addition, the *functional* relationships among the structural elements are isomorphic with that being represented. A simulation of another system therefore involves abstracting not only the static, structural relationships, but the dynamic, process relationships as well. With the incorporation of functional relations into a model, it becomes an operational and dynamic representation of *process*—a simulation. It is the exhibition of process that distinguishes simulations from such static models as blueprints, dolls, etc. (pp.11–12)

We usually think of simulation models as having something to do with the computer. For example, the work of Abelson and Bernstein (1963) in computer simulations of conflict over community referendum issues, Guetzkow's (1970) work in international relations and the development of the internation simulation program, and Gullahorn and Gullahorn's (1963) computer simulation model of elementary social behavior all utilize the computer—and a variety of programs—to operationalize their models.

Although computers have played, and will continue to play, an increasingly important role in model building, simulational models do not need a computer to be operationalized. For example, the classic "robber's cave experiment" of Sherif *et al.* (1961) simulated the effects of an emergency on the cohesiveness of a "community." Similarly, Drabek's (1969) simulation of a police radio dispatch room under different conditions of stress and information input did not rely on a computer. He used "real" police officers, "real" equipment, and modified and controlled incoming messages. The study was conducted under laboratory conditions.

The essential property of a simulation model is that components of the model be given values, relations among components be specified clearly, and instructions (e.g., rules or a computer program) be provided that sets the model into operation.

## MISCONCEPTIONS ABOUT MODELS

What is a model? At the outset of this chapter it was pointed out that there exists a wide variety of answers to this question. Some uncertainty is to be expected when deciding what type of model is needed for developing different theories. Additional uncertainty, in the form of misconception about models and the modeling process, is not needed. It is to some of these misconceptions that we now turn our attention.

Brodbeck (1968) discusses four unnecessary and confusing uses of the term *model* in the social sciences. First, the term is not used profitably to refer to an untested or untestable theory. Brodbeck says that theories which lack empirical support frequently are called models "because of a reluctance to honor them as full-fledged theories" (pp.586). Type I and II Theories sometimes are called models when the term model has less prestige than the term theory. But if a model is seen to perform a representational function and types of theories are differentiated, this misconception can be avoided.

The second unnecessary use of the term Brodbeck mentions is to define a model as a theory that consciously neglects certain variables. For example, game theory frequently is called a model because it assumes rationality in human behavior. It assumes that the individuals "playing the game" know all possible outcomes, have all relevant information, know the values placed on their own alternative choices, and their opponents' choices, and always behave to maximize their outcomes. Because this theory consciously neglects certain nonrational and emotional dimensions of man, the theory is thought to be idealistic or incomplete and is therefore called a model rather than a theory. Again, however, this is a misuse of the term model. A model should not be used to refer to an incomplete, small, or narrow theory.

A third misuse of the term model is when it refers to a theory incorporating idealized parameters. For example, if we are interested in the spread of rumors in a network, we can idealize the theory by assuming no other information is present in the network when the rumor is planted. Or we might be interested in group discussion and idealize our theory by assuming perfect information, much the same way as the physicist assumes perfect gas or frictionless bodies. Or we might be interested in the acquisition of behavioral norms in a new and novel social situation. We might idealize our theory by assuming zero previous social interaction experience. Such idealized theories, however, are not properly referred to as models of their respective forms of human behavior.

Finally, Brodbeck claims it is sloppy thinking to refer to quantified theories as models. Simply because a theory is clearly enough defined and thoroughly enough investigated to have numbers attached to its central concepts does not make it any less or any more a theory. With the first unnecessary use of the term, it was used as an apology for an incomplete theory. With the last unnecessary use Brodbeck cites, model is used to dignify a highly quantified theory.

It is important to point out that these uses of the term are not incorrect as much as they are unnecessary. If we allow the term model to have several very different referents, the term becomes meaningless. Brodbeck is making an argument for reserving the term model as a label for the representational process. The next chapter clarifies the notion of "model" further by discussing the various structures, substances, and types of models.

*. . . analogies are not "aids" to the establishment of theories; they are an utterly essential part of theories, without which theories would be completely valueless and unworthy of the name.*

**N. R. CAMPELL**   *Physics, the Elements*

# 10

# Models: Their Structures, Substances, and Types

# INTRODUCTION

In the last chapter we discussed some general issues concerning models, their construction, function and evaluation. In this chapter we will take a more detailed look at the variety of models that can be built. Earlier it was argued that the primary function of a model is to facilitate theory construction. We will now examine this function by considering three dimensions of models. Specifically, four *structures*, six *substances*, and three *types* are discussed. Any model of the social sciences can be defined on these three dimensions. The particular structures, substances, and types treated here are the most frequently relied on instances of these dimensions; others certainly exist and new instances can be formulated.

# THE STRUCTURE OF ANALOGUES

Analogues can be differentiated with respect to the types of structures characterizing them. Recall that one criterion a model-builder must satisfy is to be aware of the structural properties of the analogue being proposed as a model. The following discussion considers four different instances of structures that can characterize an analogue (see Deese, 1969).

## Hierarchical Structure

If an analogue is characterized by a hierarchical structure, the elements of the structure are arranged in a series of superordinate-subordinate relations with the total number of elements increasing as one proceeds from the top of the structure to the bottom. Figure 6 illustrates a typical hierarchical structure.

Analogues characterized by hierarchical structures are used to represent objects and processes that can be decomposed systematically into their component parts. For example, Chomsky's (1965) theory of transformational grammar is based on a model the analogue for which is hierarchical in structure. Chomsky models sentences by breaking them into noun phrases and verb phrases. Each of these phrases, in turn, is further subordinated and subdivided into its component parts (see Figure 7). Each element or node of the structure represents a set of attributes which describes the material beneath it. The lines connecting the nodes indicate the super-

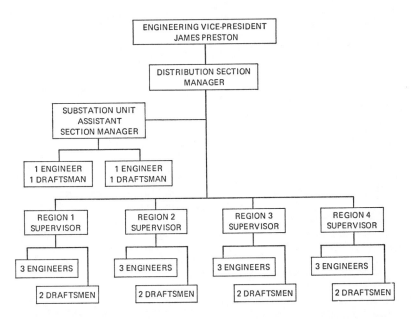

**Fig. 6** A typical hierarchical structure, here illustrating a utility power company's organizational chart. (Reprinted from John A. Seiler. *Systems Analysis in Organizational Behavior.* Homewood, Ill.: Irwin-Dorsey, 1967, p. 34.)

subordinate relations that are assumed to be valid. Thus, for example, although two or more nodes may be subordinate to another, a direct relation is not assumed to hold if the subordinate elements are not connected to the superordinate element.

Another example of analogues characterized by a hierarchical structure are those used to model the channels of communication among people in an organization. The stockholders, in a large profit-making organization, are at the pinnacle of the structure. Subordinate to the stockholders is the chairman of the board, then the board, then the president, and so on down to the lowest level personnel. Each element of the analogue now represents a formally defined organizational position and the lines represent formal channels of communication and authority.

One final example of hierarchical analogues used as models is when they represent kinship systems in cultural anthropological research. Differences between cultures, and even within cultures between status groups, can be determined by using a hierarchical analogue to model culturally recognized and acknowledged rela-

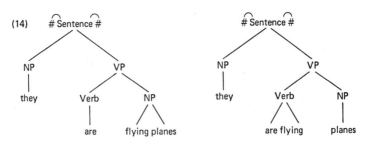

**Fig. 7** Chomsky's noun-phrase (NP)/ verb-phrase (VP) structure diagram illustrating an ambiguous sentence. The word "flying" can be used as an adjective, as in the diagram on the left, giving the sentence one meaning, or as a verb, giving the sentence a completely different meaning. (Reprinted from Noam Chomsky. Three models for the description of language. In A. G. Smith (ed.), *Communication and Culture.* New York: Holt, Rinehart and Winston, 1966, p. 147.)

tions among relatives. Again, the analogue is used, among other reasons, to model subordinate-superordinate relations and relational complexities.

**Grouping Structure**

If an analogue is characterized by a grouping structure, the elements in any given grouping are said to have two or more attributes in common. Probably the best example of a theory the model for which is a grouping structure analogue is general systems theory. General systems theory is based on the assumption that seemingly dissimilar objects and events can be grouped together insofar as they share two or more similar attributes.

Whereas hierarchical analogues force and focus on ever finer differences in attributes among objects or processes, grouping analogues force and focus on ever broader similarities among objects and processes. Although different group levels exist, as exemplified in the notion of supra-system, system, and sub-system in general systems theory, the emphasis is on finding similarities across levels and grouping them rather than finding distinctions and separating them.

Functional leadership theories of small group behavior also rest on models the analogues of which are grouping structures. These theories contend that, irrespective of the individuals enacting certain communicative behaviors, those behaviors which serve a leadership function can be grouped together and talked about in terms of a functional rather than personal role enactment.

In sociology, most theories of status-set formation rest on grouping structures. In brief, these theories posit that members of a society are aware of their differences but also are aware of how they are similar to others. Stated another way, status-set formation consists of identifying attributes you share with others, determining the saliencies of those shared attributes, and grouping yourself with others similar in those salient attributes.

## Scalar Structures

If an analogue is characterized by a scalar structure, the elements of the structure are related to each other in units of numbers, probabilities, or intensities. These units stand in scalar relation to one another. The analogue serving as the model for many decision theories is characterized by a scalar structure. Each outcome alternative is rank ordered (i.e., scaled in numerical units) in terms of subjective and objective utility (which are also scaled in numerical units) and then each alternative is assigned a probability value (probability units scaled appropriately) of being chosen under different circumstances.

In communication, the fear-appeal theories of attitude change rest on analogues with scalar structures. In those theories the units to be scaled are not number or probability units but intensity units. Various messages are scaled as being of high-intensity fear-arousal appeal, others of medium-intensity fear-arousal appeal, and others of low-intensity fear-arousal appeal. Predictions are then made about the degree (usually scaled numerically) of attitude change resulting from the presentation of these appeals.

Another example would be the theories of meaning which rely on the semantic differential as a tool for measuring the meanings of concepts. Insofar as these theories explain meaning in terms of degrees of intensity of underlying dimensions (in the case of the semantic differential these dimensions are activity, potency, and evaluation), they rest on scalar structured analogues.

Whereas hierarchical structured analogues force and focus on differences in terms of subordination and superordination (a vertical differentiating structure), scalar structured analogues force and focus on differences in terms of degree (a horizontal differentiating structure).

## Spatio-Temporal Structures

If an analogue is characterized by a spatio-temporal structure, the elements of the structure are related to one another in time and in a multidimensional space. Most theories of human interaction have as a model an analogue with a spatio-temporal structure. For example, Bales's (1950) theory of group interaction assumes that the elements (here defined as units of verbal behavior) are related in either a socio-emotional or task space and also related in time (i.e., the units of verbal behavior are related sequentially). The coordinates defined by the space and time parameters identify clusters of behavior that describe the interaction process.

Several cybernetic theories of purposive behavior also share a spatio-temporal analogue. Different modes of behavior (i.e., behavior occurring at different points in behavior space) function to clarify past behavior and redefine or focus more clearly on future objectives (the past and future here refer to behavioral time). It is the interaction of behavioral time and space, and their coordinates at any given instant, that defines the purpose of the cybernetic system.

In parapsychology, most theories of ESP and clairvoyance rest on spatio-temporal structures. In the case of clairvoyance theories, behavioral space is assumed to interact with a collapsed behavioral time; present cognitive behaviors interact with future behaviors that have "cognitively collapsed" and become part of the present to enable prediction.

## THE SUBSTANCE OF ANALOGUES

The insightful model-builder possesses a relatively broad knowledge base, embracing not only the other social sciences but some of the natural sciences, humanities, and mathematics as well. This is not to say that to build useful models one need be a renaissance man; rather it is to say that a parochial narrowness of interests and information is not conducive to identifying and formulating analogues whose logical structures function as models for theories.

The last section dealt with structures characterizing analogues; this section deals with substances characterizing analogues. These are the types of substances overlaying the logical structures. We will review six types of substances for analogues—substances whose origins range from economics to physics to medicine—that are widely used in the social sciences. In discussing the process of model building, March (1970) briefly mentions them. We will develop each in greater detail.

## Individual Choice

The first analogue substance concerns *individual choice*. March says these analogues are concerned with "the processes by which individuals choose among alternatives, make decisions, and solve problems" (p.67). Investment behavior, gambling, voting, occupational choice, consumer behavior, and the selection of friends and mates typically are the types of social behaviors treated in individual choice analogues. The analogue assumes rational or quasi-rational choice behavior. This usually means that we must assume the individual making the choice has near perfect knowledge about the alternatives available to him and that he can rank order or assign priorities to those alternatives in terms of their utility or payoff value to him.

In social psychology, for example, theories of cognitive dissonance use the individual choice analogue (as well as the *structure* analogue to be discussed later) and are particularly concerned with how the perceived utility of an alternative changes once it has been chosen (e.g., see Brehm and Cohen, 1962). In micro-economics, decision theories use the individual choice analogue (e.g., see Edwards and Tversky, 1967). Those theories are concerned with determining the subjective and objective utility values of different alternatives for an individual and then predicting subsequent choices or decisions. In communication, counterattitudinal advocacy theory uses this as an analogue of individual audience member responses to conflicting message appeals (e.g., Miller, 1973).

## Collective Choice

March says the collective choice type of analogue is used frequently to represent "the ways in which collectivities of individuals reach mutually satisfactory joint decisions. In particular, we consider such problems as choice within committees, groups, organizations, and societies" (p.68). Again, as with the individual choice analogue, rational or quasi-rational behavior is assumed in which the individuals involved have access to all relevant information and are aware of the alternatives available to them.

In management and administrative sciences, this is one of the analogues for theories of organizational optimizing (e.g., Gagné, 1962; and Catanese and Steiss, 1970). The objective of these theories is to predict the most efficient means by which an organization can utilize its resources to maximize its output or productivity. In social psychology this is an analogue for coping theories of group decision making (e.g., Kahn, Wolfe, Quinn and Snoek, 1964). These theories predict differential qualities and quantities of group decisions given different amounts of information of varying degrees of accuracy to different combinations of group members. In communication, theories of multiperson decisions in completely competitive, partially competitive, and completely cooperative situations rest on the collective choice analogue (e.g., Davis, 1970).

### Exchange

March describes this analogue as a "special case of individual and collective choice" (p.68). The exchange substance initially functioned as the analogue underlying many economic theories and later was used as the foundation for one theory of power (e.g., Blau, 1964) as well as a number of other social phenomena (Homans, 1961; Gergen, 1969). It is the basis for Gouldner's (1960) theory of reciprocity and Walton and McKersie's (1965) theory of labor negotiation.

Many theories of communication rest on exchange analogues. Berlo's (1960) theory defines a message in exchange terminology. He maintains that a sender transmits a message to a receiver who, in turn, transmits feedback cues to the original sender. In short, a message is exchanged for feedback cues.

The sizable research literature using some form of interaction analysis methodology rests on a special type of exchange analogue. What is being exchanged over time is the verbal behaviors of the interactants. Bales (1950) developed one of the most widely used sets of coding categories and his initial work on the verbal interaction of group members heralded the onset of this research effort.

Since that time, numerous social scientists have constructed category schemes for coding both verbal and nonverbal behaviors in an effort to describe and explain communicative behaviors of individuals exchanging behaviors in dyads and groups.

## Adaptation

Many theories resting on exchange analogues are also, in part, *adaptation* analogues. March says that adaptation analogues are concerned with "modification of behavior by individuals and collectivities in response to experience. . . . The ideas are applied to learning, personality development, socialization, organizational change, attitude change, and cultural change" (p.68).

Berlo's theory of communication not only assumes that messages are exchanged but also that behavior is modified by adapting to feedback cues. Most theories of communication make the adaptation assumption; it is apparent in the form of a feedback device. Messages are transmitted via the feedback loop and allow the system to modify itself and adapt to new conditions.

In other areas of the social sciences the adaptation analogue informs most theories of altruism and helping behavior (e.g., Macaulay and Berkowitz, 1970), impression formation (e.g., Goffman, 1959, 1963, 1969), role formation and change (e.g., Biddle and Thomas, 1966), behavior modification (e.g., Bandura, 1969), and socialization (e.g., Goslin, 1969). The essential idea behind the adaptation analogue is that behavior is modifiable and it does change, in a variety of ways, over time depending upon a host of variables including situation, personality, and the other's behavior patterns.

## Diffusion

The fifth analogue March calls *diffusion*. This analogue concerns "the spread of behaviors, attitudes, knowledge, and information through society. The basic models are borrowed from epidemiology and include both simulations of contact, transmission, and contagion and simple versions of differential equation models of the spread of a 'disease' over time. The models are applied to the spread of fads, innovations, rumors, political allegiances, emotions, and ideas with special attention to the effects of social structure on the patterns and rate of diffusion." (pp.68–69)

Perhaps the two most familiar theories resting on diffusion-based analogues, to students of communication, are Shibutani's (1966) study of rumor as improvised news and Rogers's (1962) and later Rogers and Shoemaker's (1971) theory of the communication of innovations in various cultural contexts. There are also a number of sociological theories of the spread of hysteria in crowds (e.g., Kerckhoff, 1970; and Lang and Lang, 1970). The central idea to this analogue is that a commodity, be it a disease, an innovation, a rumor, or hysteria, spreads over time and is not contained among a small number of persons, as is the assumption with the previously discussed analogues.

### Structure

The last analogue March discusses is that of *structure*. These analogues serve as "models for structural regularities in groups, societies, beliefs, attitudes, cognitions, and interpersonal relations. The basic model is a simple structural balance model elaborated into a more general discussion of rules for structural consistency—the 'clumping' of things. The model is applied to attitude structures, kinship structures, language structures, group structures, and cognitive structures." (p.69) The concern is with substantive structure rather than logical structure.

Theories informed by structural analogues are numerous in the social sciences. A few representative examples include Parsons's (1937) classic work on the structure of social action, Theodorson's (1961) studies of human ecology, Deutsch's (1963) study of governmental relations, Cantril's (1965) theory of the patterns of human concerns, and Barker's (1968) theory of ecological psychology.

For students of communication, Newcomb's (1953) theory of communicative acts, sociometric theories of inter-group relations (e.g., Bates and Cloyd, 1956), Heider's (1958) theory of human relationships, and theories of cognitive dissonance (e.g., those reviewed in Abelson et al., 1968) may be more familiar. The central idea of structural theories of communication is that the structure of the salient relationships is defined and maintained by communicative behaviors and/or cognitive-attitudinal structures.

Analogues, then, may have any one, or combination of, four logical structures and each logical structure may have any one, or combination of, six types of substances. This classification is by no means exhaustive. Thus, even before the model-builder strips away one substance-type and maps on another substance-type, he can select from among twenty-four basic types of analogues, defined by all the possible structure-substance combinations. The next section considers three types of models that can be built, irrespective of which structural and substantive properties the analogue may have.

## TYPES OF MODELS

### Scale Models

A scale model has two distinguishing attributes; it represents similarities among objects or processes with physical material, and it preserves the relative proportions and salient features of what is being modeled. For example, the wing span, length, and wheel size of a model airplane are scaled down according to the same proportional ratio from the airplane for which it is a scale model. In addition, the scale model airplane is made of material substance (including visual-pictorial models displayed on cathode ray tubes and "wind tested" in a computer via a simulation).

Other than these two attributes, scale models resemble conceptual and mathematical models in the following important respects. First, scale models, like all models, stand in asymmetrical relation to the object or process being modeled. The plastic toy airplane is a model for the object airplane; the real airplane cannot be a model for the object airplane.

Second, models are designed to serve some pragmatic purpose. They are not justified solely in terms of the aesthetic pleasure experienced by the model-builder during its construction. A scale model airplane is constructed because it is easier and more economical to wind test than is the "real thing." General Motors design engineers build scale models of automobiles because models are easier to modify than are production-line cars. Anatomy teachers use plastic scale models of man's muscle structure because using the "real thing" is impossible logistically or unfeasible economically.

Third, a model is used to determine the dimensions of the object or process being modeled. For example, an engineer constructs a scale model bridge to test the tensile strength of various girder configurations. NASA engineers construct scale model space capsules to determine their stability and strength under different pitch and yaw conditions.

Fourth, some features of the model are irrelevant and are not parts of the object or process being modeled. By the same token, not all parts of the real object or process have corresponding parts in the model. For example, to wind test an airplane scale model, the model need not contain the engine as long as the model weighs as much proportionally as the real airplane and the weight is distributed in the model as it is in the real plane.

By definition, there is no such thing as a model that is perfectly faithful to the real object in every detail. To build such a model would result in another identical airplane and not a scale model. Even in the instances of artificial organs (e.g., heart, kidney,), such models are not perfectly faithful to the real organ in terms of material composition, shape, or function.

The social sciences differ from the natural sciences in terms of their respective reliances on scale models. Many of the natural sciences are concerned with physical objects and processes. To the extent that a science attempts to explain physical phenomena, scale models will play an important role in theory development. But most of the social sciences are concerned with nonphysical objects and processes. Attitude formation and change, decision-making, role emergence and definition, power, and conflict are hypothetical constructs that have no physical referents. Consequently, the importance of scale models for theory development in the social sciences is minimal. Conceptual and mathematical models play much more critical roles.

## Conceptual Models

Scale models usually involve no substantive change in medium; both the object automobile and the model automobile have a similar appearance differing only in scale and, perhaps, material. Conceptual models, on the other hand, involve a change in medium. Such models, rather than representing the *outward appearances* of the object or process being modeled, represent as faithfully as possible the *internal structure* or web of relationships in the original object or process.

For example, a scale model of a five-person discussion group would be five mannequins or wax figures, similar in appearance to the people being modeled, seated around a table. A conceptual model might be a sociometric illustration of the cluster of people related by bonds of agreement and liking, the cluster of people related by bonds of disagreement and disliking, and the isolates. The structure illustrated in Figure 5 can function as a conceptual model of a small group or business conglomerate, depending upon which substance is mapped onto it. But a model airplane can only be a model of an airplane.

Maruyama's (1963) representation of population growth and diminution in an urban area is an example of a structure consisting of directional lines and nodal points. The structure models a body

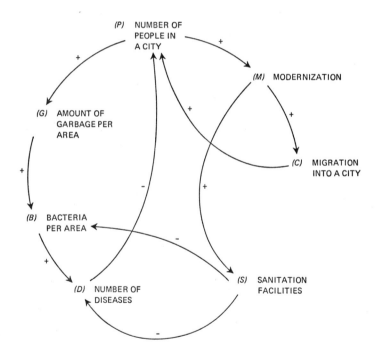

**Fig. 8** (Reprinted from Magoroh Maruyama. The second cybernetics: deviation-amplifying mutual cause processes. In W. Buckley (ed.), *Modern Systems Research for the Behavioral Sciences.* Chicago: Aldine, 1968, p. 311.)

of information about urban population dynamics. These bodies of information (e.g., census data, epidemiological data, migration data,) are combined and their underlying structure or interrelationship is represented or modeled. The + signs indicate a direct relationship between the concepts connected by the directional line and the − signs indicate an inverse relationship. Starting with any concept, one can determine how the system operates by tracing the direct or inverse relationships connecting the component concepts.

Both scale and conceptual models are symbolic representations of some object or process and both have rules of correspondence. These rules enable us to draw inferences from the model that pertain to the object or process being modeled. As we said earlier, a model is not a completely faithful representation of the object it is modeling; certain details are systematically left out. The model-builder must provide the model-user with rules for how the model corresponds to the original being modeled so that accurate uses of the model can be made.

It is with respect to the rules of correspondence that a scale model and a conceptual model differ. Scale models are judged according to their degree of *external/physical similarity* to the object modeled. Conceptual models are judged according to their degree of *internal/structural similarity* to the object or process modeled. The better the model, the closer it corresponds to the original in certain important respects. A more precise way of stating that idea, with respect now to conceptual models, is that there is a point-by-point correspondence between the key internal/structural relations in the original and in the model.

Going back to our example of a discussion group, if we are interested in modeling the interpersonal relationships connecting the group members, the model must include the various dimensions of that internal/structure (i.e., liking, disliking, coalitions, isolates). The model must include rules for translating it back to the original. Mathematicians call the point-by-point correspondence of two or more objects or processes an isomorphism. We are talking here about close correspondence or a high degree of isomorphism between two objects or processes but not an identity relationship.

A conceptual model is more abstract, i.e., further removed from the physical world, than is a scale model. Because conceptual models are more abstract than scale models, conceptual models may apply to a wider range of original objects and processes than may scale models. For example, suppose we found that the structure of relationships among different element particles in a certain magnetic field was quite similar to the structure of relationships among people with different personalities in a group discussion. It would be possible to represent both original objects with the same conceptual model, assuming a close fit to the rules of correspondence. But a scale model of a group discussion could hardly be used as a model of elements in a magnetic field.

The conceptual model is so named because it is an analogy of something quite different physically. The model captures an abstract conceptual feature of the object—its internal structure—and thereby creates unity from disunity. Whereas before there was no similarity between, say, elements in a magnetic field and people in a discussion group, there now is. The model represents the conceptual similarity amidst physical dissimilarities.

## Mathematical Models

Mathematics is a language; it has a vocabulary and a syntax. The language of mathematics is different from natural language, however, in several respects. In natural language, signs usually function as symbols and our interest in and use of those symbols is semantic. One symbol can have different referents to the same and different people. Consequently, we speak of natural language as being both rich and imprecise in meaning.

Mathematical language, on the other hand, treats signs as signs, devoid of specific referents, and is concerned with how signs are and can be related. In short, mathematical language is a syntactic use of signs. General semantics is the study of language concerned with *how words mean* (a semantic emphasis) whereas structural linguistics is concerned with *how words are related* (a syntactic emphasis). In this sense, structural linguistics is a more mathematical or formal study than is general semantics.

As a language, mathematics is an extremely precise way of talking about syntactic relations among signs. These signs need not have a referent because the signs are abstract entities and not names of specific objects or processes. Letters and numbers are the signs of the language of mathematics. They can represent combinations of objects or processes, providing that the relations among the signs stipulated by the mathematical sentence are true of the particular objects or processes that are substituted.

Mathematical sentences take the form of equations. Equations stipulate the relations among the signs. It is these stipulated relations that define the structure, form, or syntax of the signs involved. The reason social scientists are interested in using the language of mathematics to construct models for social structures and processes is because the language is so precise, economic, and general. An equation taking up less than one line on a page, when translated into natural language, may require paragraphs or even volumes.

Furthermore, if a model can be constructed using mathematical language, all of the mathematical operations and transformations should apply to the content being modeled. Trying out all feasible transformations may suggest relations that would not have been apparent when the model was constructed in natural language. If the mathematical sentences are indeed accurate descriptions of the process or object being modeled, then permissable transformations should produce acceptable sentences also. These mathematical transformations are the rules of correspondence for the mathematical model. They tell us how we can interpret and test the model being proposed.

When we construct a conceptual model, another object or process, supposedly sharing a common structure, is used as an analogue. In constructing a mathematical model, an equation or set of equations is the analogue. The content or object system supposedly sharing the structure of the equations is mapped onto those equations to test the fit. Signs in the equation(s) are replaced with substantive concepts. The test is to determine if what is true of the abstract equation(s) is also true of the content-filled equation(s).

When a mathematical model is constructed, some original body of substantive information is mapped onto an abstract domain of sets and functions. The substantive information is said to have been formalized. This process of formalizing substantive data is nearly identical with the process of building formal theory. The difference between a formal theory and a mathematical model is difficult to articulate; it is sufficient to say that the difference is in how they are constructed and used, not in how they look as completed products.

The advantages of constructing mathematical models for social processes lie in the resulting precision with which testable relations can be formulated and tested, the ease of deducing hypotheses by using mathematical transformations, and the clarity of the structures revealed in the object or process being modeled. If the object can be mapped onto some equation(s), the relations are more precisely stated than they are when stated linguistically. Furthermore, what relations in the object should and can be tested are more readily ascertainable when the object is represented mathematically rather than linguistically. Finally, we are able to understand and intuitively grasp the underlying structure of the object or process more easily in mathematical than natural language.

There are some serious limitations of mathematical models, however, that must be weighed against their advantages. Drastic simplifications must be made in the object being modeled before it can be mapped onto an equation or family of equations. Sometimes very stringent assumptions must be made before it is possible to map the object. Usually the variables or concepts of the object or process to be mapped must be measurable yielding at least interval data.

Given the relative youth of the social sciences, these disadvantages of mathematical models are of no small consequence. Few of the social science disciplines have developed sufficiently sophisticated measuring instruments for key variables to yield interval or ratio data. Perhaps experimental learning psychology and micro- and macro-economics are the most advanced in this respect. Indeed, many of the social science disciplines have not yet satisfactorily defined their key variables, much less developed sensitive measuring instruments for them.

There is a risk also that once we know something of mathematical models we will become so enamored of them we will try to use them in totally inappropriate circumstances. As Black (1962) points out, there is a temptation to confuse mathematical precision with the strength of empirical verification (p.225). Mapping poorly obtained data onto a mathematical equation does not improve the data. Quite to the contrary, such an activity, to the extent it is even possible, will reveal the weakness in the data in a most glaring fashion.

## TYPOLOGY OF MODELS

By this time you are probably becoming aware of the wide variety of models that can be developed. As we have defined models, they are three-dimensional tools used to facilitate theory construction. Models are analogues characterized by a *structure* and *substance* that can be built into one of three *forms*. We have discussed four types of structures and six types of substances that can characterize an analogue, and three forms in which models can be built. There certainly are more types of structures, substances, and forms for models than those we have discussed in this chapter. In the social sciences, however, the ones treated are probably the most prominent.

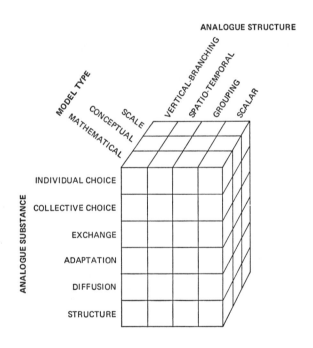

**Fig. 9** Three-dimensional typology representing seventy-two different forms of models. Any one of these models is defined by the substance of its underlying analogue and by the type of model fashioned.

Simply considering the dimensional units we have discussed, seventy-two different types of models are logically possible. Figure 9 illustrates this three-dimensional typology. Each cell represents a logically possible model form. Keep in mind that more classifications could be stipulated on each of the three dimensions, thus increasing the number of possible model types. Furthermore, to each structure-type can be mapped a wide variety of substantive materials which replace the original six substance-types we discussed as characterizing the analogue.

The rather obvious conclusion to be drawn is that there is no one "right" model to facilitate our theory construction activity. Rather, there is a confusingly large number of possible models that can be built. The type of model sought depends upon the specific needs and purposes of the theory builder. The challenge in the doing of social science is to be aware of the theoretical state of a given interest domain and to be able to build a model appropriate to that state so the model functions to further develop the theory.

*If I have so much emphasized the importance of scientific models and archetypes, it is because of a conviction that the imaginative aspects of scientific thought have in the past been too much neglected. For science, like the humanities, like literature, is an affair of the imagination.*

MAX BLACK   *Models and Metaphors*

**11**

# Descriptive Models of Communication

## INTRODUCTION

The last two chapters discuss seven different examples of communication models. This chapter considers three models whose primary function is to describe a particular feature of the communication process. Chapter 12 focuses on four models whose function is more limited in scope—to explicate a key concept of some theory. Generally speaking, descriptive models are weaker than explicative models when evaluated in terms of heuristics, isomorphism, and correspondence. The models discussed in these remaining two chapters were selected to illustrate why this is so.

More specifically, each of the models is described in terms of the rationale provided for its construction, the structure of the underlying analogue, the type of model resulting from mapping new substance onto the structure, how the model functions to build theory, and how well the model satisfies the three evaluative criteria. There exists a wide variety of models from which to choose examples. The reasons for selecting the seven appearing in these two chapters are more pragmatic than conceptual—to give you a feel for the diversity of available models and to illustrate the strengths and weaknesses of descriptive and explicative models.

## WESTLEY AND MACLEAN'S MODEL OF MASS COMMUNICATION

Westley and MacLean (1957, pp.31–38) make two distinctions between face-to-face communication and mass communication. First, face-to-face communication involves more sense modalities than mass communication. Visual cues, paralinguistic cues, olfactory cues, and kinesthetic cues are available to the participants in face-to-face communication but not available in a mass communication situation. Second, in face-to-face communication the participants have access to immediate feedback from the receiver whereas in mass communication the feedback is delayed, if present at all.

The rationale Westley and MacLean provide for constructing this model of mass communication is to highlight these differences between the two modes of communication. Newcomb's (1953) theory of communicative acts is used as the analogue for the model. Newcomb is concerned with explaining the relationships between two or more individuals and an object. He stipulates that the people involved in the communicative act must be in one another's presence and the object must be familiar to both of them.

Westley and MacLean argue that in mass communication situations the people involved are not in one another's presence and the object may not be familiar to them. Figure 10 is the authors' illustration of their model. When person B cannot receive the information about other persons and objects he needs to orient himself to his environment, he must rely on a gatekeeper (C) to select relevant information from the environment and pass it on to him. The gatekeeper in this model is the mass media and it functions to select and transmit information otherwise unavailable to B. The mass media, insofar as it functions as a gatekeeper, survives only if it satisfies B's needs for information to orient himself to his surroundings. In a sense, the function of the mass media is to extend selectively people's information environments.

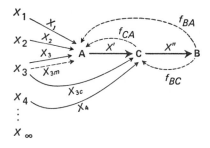

**Fig. 10** The messages C transmits to B ($X''$) represent his selections from both messages to him from As ($X'$) and C's selections and abstractions from $X$s in his own sensory field ($X_{3C}$, $X_4$), which may or may not be $X$s in A's field. Feedback not only moves from B to A ($f_{BA}$) and from B to C ($f_{BC}$) but also from C to A ($f_{CA}$). Clearly, in the mass communication situation, a large number of Cs receive from a very large number of As and transmit to a vastly larger number of Bs, who simultaneously receive from other Cs. (Reprinted from Bruce H. Westley and Malcolm S. MacLean, Jr. (1965). A conceptual model for communications research. In James H. Campbell and Hal W. Hepler (eds.). *Dimensions in Communication.* Belmont, Calif.: Wadsworth, p. 60.)

The authors argue that one of the advantages of their model is its generality. For example, B may be one person, a group of persons, or a society. The gatekeeping function, C, may be any form of mass media. They also contend that unintentional acts are objects, Xs, whereas intentional acts are As, or specific senders. The model represents communication occurring without the presence of a sender transmitting intentional messages to specific receivers. The gatekeeper transmits Xs to Bs in the absence of As. The gatekeeper is a conduit for messages rather than the source of messages per se.

## Structure

The structure of the analogue Westley and MacLean use as the basis for their model is difficult to determine. Recall that an analogue can be thought to have one of four structures; hierarchical, grouping, scalar, and spatio-temporal. Given these options, the analogue's structure most closely resembles grouping. Recall that a group structure is characterized by elements having two or more attributes in common. In the case of Newcomb's theory of communicative acts, which Westley and MacLean use as their analogue, individuals are not completely isomorphic in terms of interests and information. But these two elements do share the common attribute of object X. In the Westley and MacLean model, the Bs have C in common, although they may not share other attributes. The Cs do not have all Xs or all Bs in common but they do share some of these attributes. This way of thinking about the analogue qualifies it as a grouping structure.

It should be pointed out, however, that the authors do not make the structure of their analogue apparent. This failure to clarify the first step of model construction decreases the probability of the final model satisfying the evaluative criteria. The model is less likely to be heuristic, isomorphic, and interpretable.

## Substance

Recall that the substance of an analogue can be described in one of six ways: individual choice; collective choice; exchange; adaptation; diffusion; and structure. Westley and MacLean's model is described best as an exchange analogue. The C selects Xs from the environment and transmits them to Bs. In exchange, the Bs continue to use

C's services as a medium. This exchange relationship continues only as long as C provides the Bs with $X$s they can use to orient to their environment.

It should be noted that the substance of the original Newcomb theory is structural rather than exchange in nature. Newcomb's concern is with the balance structure of the relationship between two or more people, A and B, vis-à-vis some object $X$. The $X$ is not exchanged; rather, A and B adjust their attitudes about one another and/or about $X$ to ensure that the structure of their relationship is balanced. Newcomb uses elementary algebra to explicate his concept of a balanced structure. None of this balance substance appears in Westley and MacLean's model. To say this is not to criticize their model. It simply points out that the substance of an analogue can be transformed when it is used as a model for another theory. Westley and MacLean retained the grouping structure of Newcomb's theory, which they used as their analogue, but they changed the substance of the analogue, which is to be expected.

## Type

The title of their article correctly identifies the type of model the authors constructed; it is conceptual as opposed to scale or mathematical. Recall that the medium of a conceptual model is natural language; the medium of a scale model is a substantive material; and the medium of a mathematical model is mathematical language. Clearly, Westley and MacLean's model is not a scale model. Nor is it a mathematical model, not because it represents the internal structure of relationships among objects, gatekeepers, and receivers, but because it is explicated in natural rather than mathematical language.

## Function

This model is descriptive rather than explicative or simulative in function. Westley and MacLean are describing the general process by which persons to whom certain types of information is not available receive that information from a gatekeeper in the absence of the original source. For the model to be explicative it would have to focus on one or two central concepts of a theory and more specifically define and describe its working properties. For the model to be simulative, it would have to represent the gatekeeping process over a period of time and account for how changes in certain parameter values influence this process.

## Evaluation

Recall that an effective model must satisfy three evaluative criteria; it must be heuristic (suggest insightful questions and testable hypotheses that facilitate the development of theory), it must be isomorphic to the object or process being modeled (the material being modeled must fit relatively closely the structure of the analogue in specified ways), and the rules of correspondence must be articulated so that appropriate interpretations can be made.

The authors do not outline any questions or hypotheses their model suggests. Nor has there been a sizable amount of research stimulated directly by their model. The authors tell us very little about the critical parameters of their model so that we might speculate on how changes in these parameter values might influence the process. The model does satisfy the isomorphism criterion relatively well, although how well is difficult to determine because so little research is based on it. However, it does seem to be one plausible way of representing the gatekeeping function of mass media.

The authors are clear about their mapping procedures. We know what each of the letters represents although they do not tell us specifically how they are similar to and different from the referents for the symbols in the analogue. But more importantly, there is very little to interpret from the model. Few rules of correspondence are necessary, apart from identifying the referents for the symbols, because the model has so few apparent implications for researchable questions.

## ROSENFIELD'S GAME MODEL OF HUMAN COMMUNICATION

Rosenfield's (1968, pp.26–41) model was presented at the 1968 University of Minnesota Symposium in Speech-Communication. The symposium addressed itself to the question of what rhetoric (communication theory) is appropriate for contemporary speech communication. His answer is in the form of a model of interpersonal communication. Rosenfield argues that Aristotle "held two notions of rhetoric: the kind he wrote a book about and a kind which was apparently common in ancient Greece but which he mentioned only in passing" (p.27). It is this latter rhetoric for which Rosenfield constructs his model.

He begins by articulating four axioms pertaining to Aristotelian rhetorical theory.

1.   It is limited to language employed as a feature of social activity, whether in a personal or public context.

2.   It has no serious interest in what we call information transmission, or the field of semantics. (Here Rosenfield's thinking departs sharply from the Westley and MacLean model). Definitions of rhetoric such as "informative and suasory discourse," or "the means by which we employ language to relate ideas to men and men to ideas" both have honorable traditions, but I would argue that except under the broadest interpretation of "suasory" these approaches are at odds with what Aristotle knew rhetoric to be in his own age. Closer to the Greek conception of rhetoric may be that branch of semiotic which Charles Morris calls "Pragmatics," the way in which verbal icons relate of their users.

3.   In the instant when the rhetorical act is consummated, a large component of behavior is habit-dominated and in no wise deliberate.

4.   A fundamental component by Aristotelian rhetoric is its view that discourse is a means by which humans relate to each other. (p.28)

Rosenfield's interpretation of Aristotelian rhetoric is very contemporary and similar, in many respects, to Watzlawick, Beavin, and Jackson's (1967) theory of the pragmatics of human communication. Rosenfield contends that the most insightful way of describing his interpretation of Aristotelian rhetoric is via a game model. Central to his model are the key concepts of *rule, tactic,* and *custom*.

According to Rosenfield, a *rule* both regulates and constitutes behavior. In their constitutive function, rules operate as a system to define the behavior which, by definition, constitutes the game. For example, a touchdown in football is constituted quite literally by the rules that define the behaviors of taking an ellipsoid object across predetermined lines on an area of ground which all agree to be the

legitimate area for playing the game. Similarly, a wedding is constituted by the bride and groom giving predetermined answers to
predetermined questions posed by a legally approved third party.
Any additional behavioral trappings are customary (which will be
discussed shortly) rather than constitutive. The argument is that
rhetoric, like games, is a rule-regulated as well as a constituted
activity.

Rosenfield contends that rules possess qualities that allow
them to perform the constitutive function of reifying social institutions. In other words, rules guide behaviors the patterns of which
constitute what we refer to in everyday language as social institutions. In this respect, Rosenfield's model is quite similar to several
of Duncan's (1968) theoretical statements in his theory of social
order discussed in Chapter 5. Rules are arbitrary rather than natural; there is no natural or inherent reason why a football game
consists of four rather than two or six equal time periods. In fact,
as Rosenfield points out, sandlot football games can have any number of players and periods mutually acceptable to the participants.
Rules are arbitrary and are whatever the players of the game agree
to.

Similar to athletic games, conversational games presuppose a
unique but arbitrary set of rules. A conversation is defined by an
arbitrary set of permissive rules that, if violated, change the specific
game being played. This example brings out another of Rosenfield's points about rules; they specify limits which are intended to
prohibit likely infractions. They are seldom exhaustive or precise;
there are no rules in football against swimming across the goal line
with the football for scoring a touchdown. The rules do not include
this infraction because it is not a likely event to occur.

A fourth attribute of rules is that no one is primarily interested
in them per se or in their enforcement. They form a regulatory
backdrop against which the game is played. As Rosenfield points
out, there are no fans of umpires, only fans of game players. Rules
are noticed only when they are violated.

Because rules are arbitrary creations mutually agreed to, they
are subject to modification. But they usually remain stable during
any one enactment of a game, thus allowing the participants to
complete the game smoothly. After its completion, players may
discuss rule changes. Rosenfield concludes his discussion of rules
by stating that it is the power rules have of constituting an institu-

tion that makes them logically essential for rhetorical activity to exist.

*Tactic* is the second central concept of Rosenfield's game model of human communication. What makes a game different from a natural occurrence, he argues, is that games always have some mechanism which eventuates in an outcome or conclusion. For an activity to be a game, there must be some legitimate way for it to be concluded and for this conclusion to be recognized mutually by all participants. It is the very nature of a game to reach toward an end point.

Rosenfield defines a tactic as a behavior pattern which conforms to the rules and, at the same time, seems to be a viable means of terminating the game. In this respect, there are teleological or purpose-based standards of appropriateness that distinguish between rule violations and tactically "strange" behaviors. If we define behaviors as violations of rules we become insenced and call that behavior cheating. If we define behavior as being nonteleological or nonpurposive in terms of trying to bring the game to an end, we are puzzled and call that behavior foolish.

In terms of research and analysis, Rosenfield argues that from the game model perspective an utterance rather than traditional linguistic units, such as sentences and words, are the minimal units of tactical analysis. An utterance, according to the author, need not describe or report an object or event. An utterance itself may be the totality of a social act. In short, utterances have a performative or pragmatic dimension totally apart from their semantic- or information-transmitting function. An utterance may be its own justification for existing.

Tactical components of games correspond to the performative or instrumental character of communication. If conversation is a game, then tactics include utterances such as promises, apologies, threats, and insults. Rosenfield maintains that the instrumental function of language takes priority over the referential function in most rhetorical or communicative situations. This rule of correspondence necessitates thinking of language as social gesture. It is the performative conception of utterances that makes them tactical, as Rosenfield defines that concept.

The third important concept of the game model is *custom*. This concept the author defines as a residue of attendant patterns peripheral to the essence of the game. Cheerleaders are neither necessary nor sufficient for a game called football to be played. But they are attendant patterns of behavior without which one would sense "something is missing" from the enactment of the game. Rosenfield further defines custom by making the following distinctions: whereas tactics are teleological or purposive, customs derive their justification from tradition and habit. In the case of the conversational game, he contends that customs do abide as a distinct element of such transactions.

Probably the most useful characteristic of the game model of human communication is that the game analogue allows humans to engage in a matrix of social relationships. Along this line, Rosenfield concludes his description of the model by posing some researchable areas suggested by the model. First, he says, "I believe that in the exploration of moral-relational qualities inherent in communicative transactions lie some of our most exciting future research possibilities" (p.37). For example, election games can be played according to debate and circus rules or according to tanks-against-the-palace rules. Each rule-set implies very different moral-relational qualities.

Other research questions he provides follow. "Or consider how we might explore informal verbal exchanges—what might be the moral significance of polite conversation which maintains for us a set of acquaintances? And how does polite conversation shape our network of human contacts in ways which are different from the intimate yet exhilarating communication of lovers? These are some of the issues which to my mind will demand unraveling in the years to come." (p.38)

### Structure

The structure of the analogue for Rosenfield's model is *spatio-temporal.* Games, by their very nature, have a beginning, middle, and end. A game is defined by its playing and it is the playing in a space and over a period of time from beginning to end that gives the game analogue its spatio-temporal structure. Rules are relatively static but the tactics are patterns of behavior enacted within the rule structure whose purpose is to bring the game to an end.

### Substance

The substance of the game analogue is *collective choice.* Recall that March (1970) says collective choice analogues are used to represent "the ways in which collectivities of individuals reach mutually satisfactory joint decisions. In particular, we consider such problems as choice within committees, groups, organizations, and societies." (p.68)

Although collective choice analogues assume rational or quasirational behavior, Rosenfield's game model satisfies that assumption. Given a set of rules which constitute a game and regulate behavior, the individual players choose tactics with the purpose of bringing the game to a successful conclusion. Within the rule structure, then, human behavior is quasi-rational. Clearly, games involve joint or collective choices to agree on the nature of the game they are playing; that is, the nature of the rules which will regulate their behavior.

## Type

The type of model Rosenfield constructs from the game analogue is *conceptual.* The language he uses is natural rather than mathematical.

## Function

The function of the model is to *describe* rather than explicate or simulate. Rosenfield constructs the model to represent a conception of rhetoric which he claims was operative in Aristotle's contemporary society but about which he did not write. Furthermore, this model of rhetoric or communication is contemporary. In a sense, this rhetoric is the rhetoric of everyday social interaction made possible by man's ability to use language. This language is used in the everyday world primarily for its performative function and it is this function that is most gamelike. This form of social interaction is contemporary to every society. Although the content of the conversational games may change, conversational games provide the logic and structure for our everyday world, at whatever point in time that world exists.

## Evaluation

The game model of human communication fares slightly better than the Westley and MacLean model of mass communication in terms of satisfying the three evaluative criteria. First, the model is sufficiently novel and insightful to produce a wide variety of researchable questions. Rosenfield mentions only a few of these questions at the end of his article, however. There are certainly several other sets of plausible questions the model suggests. How much actual research this particular model has produced is a difficult question to answer. Certainly the work of Goffman (1959, 1963, 1969), Sudnow, (1972), Labov (1966), to name a few, uses an implicit or explicit game model for human interaction. If to satisfy the *heuristic* criterion, however, all that must be shown is that this is a model-type that has been used by others, then it must be concluded that the game model of human communication is relatively heuristic.

The *isomorphism* criterion is less well satisfied. Rosenfield works hard to demonstrate the similarities between certain athletic games, particularly football, and certain communication or conversational games. But beyond general shared characteristics, such as both having rules and using tactics to bring the activity to a conclusion, more detailed identities remain unspecified.

Perhaps the *correspondence* criterion fares the poorest. At times Rosenfield seems more interested in explicating the key concepts of the model than in mapping rhetorical substance onto his spatio-temporal analogue. Consequently, if we were to identify particular types of verbal tactics in an argument, for example, Rosenfield provides few rules for us to follow and subsequently test our mapping procedures.

## BECKER'S MOSAIC MODEL OF MESSAGE ENVIRONMENTS

Becker (1968, pp.9–25) delivered a paper at the same symposium that produced Rosenfield's model. Becker argues that more communication scholars should be developing macro-theory to complement the energy devoted to the development of micro-theory. He contends that much effort is devoted to studying the effects of single isolated messages on well-defined audiences. Relatively few studies exist focusing on the effects of multiple and diffuse messages presented repeatedly over time to a large and constantly changing audience.

Becker's argument is that we are exposed repeatedly to sets of messages in our everyday lives. Yet very few studies have been conducted to assess the effects of such messages on both attitudes and overt behaviors. To represent more adequately the message environment in which we constantly find ourselves, Becker constructs a model using McLuhan's metaphor of the television as a mosaic mesh of light and dark spots. An illustration of Becker's mosaic is presented in Figure 11. The mosaic consists of infinite message bits on any given topic. These bits are scattered over time, space, and modes of communication. Each cell of the mosaic has the potential of containing a message pertaining to any given topic. The blanked cells represent an absence of a message.

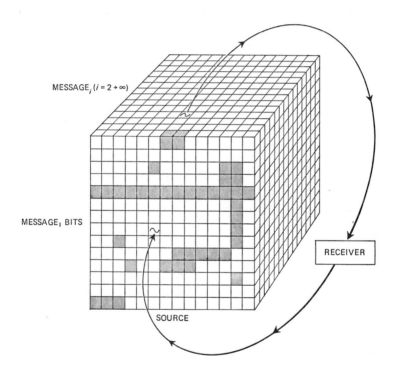

**Fig. 11** Becker's mosaic model of human communication. (Reprinted from Samuel L. Becker (1968). Toward an appropriate theory for contemporary speech-communication. In David H. Smith (ed.), *What Rhetoric (Communication Theory) Is Appropriate for Contemporary Speech Communication?* The Proceedings of the University of Minnesota Spring Symposium in Speech-Communication, 17.)

Becker begins by describing how he learned of the death of Martin Luther King, Jr. He got the story in pieces from very different sources over a relatively short period of time. He maintains that although this particular example is more compressed in time than the way we learn about many other phenomena, it is still representative of the basic processes at work. The mosaic is one's total message environment.

The model represents two processes; first, the ever-increasing number and variety of messages and their sources, and second, the repetitiveness of going through the same or similar transactions again and again. Becker is asking us to think of the mosaic as a changing cube through which the receiver is constantly moving. Some of the cells are empty because at any point in time some messages are not available from some sources. Each vertical slice or layer of the mosaic represents a particular message set. For example, the front slice might represent messages about the King murder. The other slices of the mosaic represent other message sets, for example, Watergate, the energy crisis. The cells represent the messages. The receiver goes through cells of the mosaic in continuous loops. The frequency of the loops varies; some people expose themselves to messages more frequently than others; some expose themselves to a wider variety of messages than others.

Becker acknowledges that one of the problems with the model is operationally defining a message. He admits that the mosaic can be broken down several different ways and the problem is to discover which of the operational definitions is practical and theoretically useful.

The author concludes his article by outlining some of the questions the mosaic model generates. One exemplary question Becker poses focuses on the communication processes operating to give the young black in the ghetto the information and motivation for continuing high school or dropping out. To answer this question, several smaller questions must be posed and answered. For example, what is the relevant set of message bits, what is the mosaic available to him, what is the probability of exposure and reexposure to each bit from each source, what are the structures of the message bits, and how do these structures interact with the factors to influence action? (Pp. 19–20)

Other researchable questions involve characteristics of the message per se. For example, it would be possible to measure redundancy, organization, emphasis, rate, context, and consistency of message bits. Becker concludes his article by discussing some research strategies for answering these questions.

## Structure

The analogue for Becker's model—McLuhan's mosaic mesh of light and dark spots—can be said to have a *grouping* structure. McLuhan's mosaic mesh is not developed theoretically to the point of allowing Becker to make inferences from the analogue to the model he constructs from it. Consequently, the heuristic value of the structure of the analogue used for the model is minimal. But the structure of the model is grouping insofar as the item of interest in the model is the cell representing the message from a certain source. How these messages are grouped with one another forming a mosaic cube through which the receiver passes is what characterizes the structure of the analogue.

## Substance

The substance of the analogue is even of less use to Becker than was a knowledge of its structure. McLuhan argues that the television medium is different from the film medium insofar as the former consists of a mosaic mesh of light and dark spots and the viewer must fill in the dark spots, make connections among dots, and thereby arrive at an image. Becker makes little, if any, use of this particular substance.

In one sense, the substance of the analogue can be thought of as diffusion insofar as the mosaic cube consists of different messages from different sources on different issues, and these messages change over time. The receiver, in passing through the mosaic of messages, passes through different cells on subsequent "trips" through his message environment. It is not a diffusion analogue insofar as the receiver does not diffuse information to others, at least this aspect is not stressed in Becker's model.

The mosaic analogue can also be thought of as having substance representing the *structure* of the environment. In this sense, the analogue's substance is structural. It is the structural configuration of the cells of messages and the relation of each vertical slice of the mosaic cube that influences the behavior of the receiver passing through the mosaic.

## Type

Becker's model, like Rosenfield's and Westley and MacLean's, is *conceptual*. Becker is providing a somewhat different conceptual vocabulary for thinking about message environments than existed previously. There is no attempt to utilize mathematical language, although future statements about the mosaic conceivably could be mathematical expressions. It is also possible to develop a scale model of the mosaic, but the heuristic value of such an activity is questionable.

## Function

The function of the model is *descriptive* rather than explicative or simulative. Becker is attempting to describe how people come into contact with messages and gather information during daily activities. He is providing an alternative to the rather limited notion of people receiving isolated messages complete in themselves and receiving them only once. The possibilities for simulating the process are apparent. But before simulation is possible, certain key concepts will have to be explicated. Becker identifies one of the key concepts in need of more precise explication; the concept of a message bit. One way of thinking about a simulation model of the mosaic message environment idea is that several explicative models must be developed first. Once central concepts are more clearly represented, these concepts can be given values and the process becomes possible to model simulatively.

## Evaluation

Becker's model is of questionable merit when set over against the evaluative criteria. There is little question that the model is *heuristic*. The questions he lists at the end of his article are provocative and certainly are generated from the model. The serious question is how *isomorphic* the structure of the model is to the structure of the substance being mapped onto it. For example, as Becker represents the sender it is possible for him to completely leave the mosaic of message bits and reenter at different frequencies, as well as pass through the mosaic at different rates. But is it plausible that anyone ever removes himself from his message environment? What are some examples of individuals receiving absolutely no messages on any topic from any source at any time period? Might it not be more isomorphic to think of the receiver constantly moving around in different patterns within the mosaic rather than entering and leaving it at various times? These are questions pertaining to the isomorphism of the model and the process being modeled.

The third criterion pertains to the *rules of correspondence.* How clearly does Becker translate the substance being modeled into the terms of the model? An answer to this question brings us back to the issue of operationally defining the key concepts of the model. What is a message or message bit? How frequently do the bits in the cells change? Does the size of the mosaic change and if so why and in response to what kinds of conditions? If the model were maximally testable, the reader would have answers to all or some of these questions which pertain directly to how the model is to be interpreted. Interpretation would be easier if the rules of correspondence were specified more clearly.

With some idea of the strengths and weaknesses of the three descriptive models in mind, we now proceed to consider three explicative models and one simulative model. Keep in mind that perhaps the most generally shared strength of descriptive models is that they are heuristic. However, in terms of their "goodness of fit" with the substance being mapped onto the structures and the clarity of the procedures for mapping the new conceptual substance, descriptive models usually leave much to be desired.

*We must bring science back into life as a human enterprise, an enterprise that has at its core the uncertainty, the flexibility, the subjectivity, the sweet unreasonableness, the dependence upon creativity and faith which permit it, when properly understood, to take its place as a friendly and understanding companion to all the rest of life.*

**WARREN WEAVER**  *The Imperfections of Science*

# 12

# Explicative and Simulative Models of Communication

## INTRODUCTION

The format used in the last chapter for presenting the three descriptive models will be used in this chapter in discussing three explicative models and one simulative model. The simulative model, Holder and Ehling's (1967) information decision model, is included primarily for purposes of comparison; the reader should finish this chapter with a clearer understanding of the differences among the three types of models discussed. The reason for not including more examples of simulative models is that very few have been developed; very few that model communicative behavior, that is. But the one selected provides a good example of this type of model.

## EXPLICATIVE MODEL: FISHER AND HAWES'S INTERACT SYSTEM MODEL

In response to the criticisms of several students of small group behavior (e.g., Bormann, 1970; Gouran, 1970; McGrath and Altman, 1966), Fisher and Hawes (1971) developed a model that represents the small group as an open system. Much of the criticism centered on the lack of focus in small group research and the lack of attention to process characteristics of small group behavior over time. The authors use general system theory as their analogue and define several pivotal concepts. A *system* is defined as a set of interdependent units. It is the interdependence that enables a cluster of individual units to function as one. This is defined as the *holistic* principle of systems.

A *closed system* is one whose boundaries seal the components off from the surrounding environment. In short, the environment has no interactive effect on the system because the system's boundaries are impermeable. The natural tendency for closed systems is to atrophy or disintegrate over time. The components become increasingly unrelated over time; the interdependence of the system lessens until finally the individual components no longer constitute a system.

An *open system,* on the other hand, is a set of interrelated components that are influenced by their surrounding environment. The boundaries of an open system are permeable, consequently the effects of the environment do influence the nature of the interdependency of the components. An open system has the potential of becoming more complex, remaining stable, or atrophying over time. A closed system can only proceed in one direction; toward disintegration.

The Fisher and Hawes model represents small groups as open systems that are affected by their surrounding environment. Unlike the authors of other open system models of small groups, however, Fisher and Hawes map the conceptual substance of small groups onto the open system structure differently. Most models represent an individual group member as the component, and a group (defined as two or more individuals) as the system. Fisher and Hawes define units of verbal behavior as components of the system and the system is all verbal behavior required in solving a problem. Rather than being interested in social-psychological variables that are said to connect the individual group members, Fisher and Hawes are interested in the organization, patterning, structure, or syntax of the sequence of verbal behavior. General system models that represent individual group members as components and the group as the system are defined as Human System Models; their model, which represents utterances as components and the discussion as the system, is called the Interact System Model.

The rationale given for developing the model is that no such model exists and it has the potential not only of generating new research questions and hypotheses but also of integrating previous findings that appear unrelated. Fisher and Hawes define the smallest unit of the system as an act; i.e., one single utterance uninterrupted by any other utterance. These components are combined into interacts which are pairs of contiguous verbal utterances. Double interacts are combinations of three contiguous verbal utterances. The statistical patterning of these components is the object of interest.

The model has three different conceptual levels. First is the level of the interact. At level two, these components define identifiable phases of communication. When statistical regularities in the patterning or organization of the interact components change, the system has moved into a different phase of operation. Phases are defined operationally as a change in the statistical patterning of the component interacts. Third is the level of cycles. The authors hypothesize that in processing any given task, the verbal utterances can be described as proceeding through a definite sequence of phases. When a new task or problem needs processing, the verbal utterances combine into phases and the phases pass through a cycle defining task completion. In short, contiguous pairs of verbal utterances are defined as interacts, clusters of interacts are defined as phases, and characteristic sequences of phases are defined as cycles.

Fisher and Hawes point out that their model is assumed to overlap and be complementary to different Human System Models. The Human System Model provides the researcher with an array of structural independent variables such as cohesiveness, task complexity, leadership style, and amount of initial information. The Interact System Model provides the researcher with a way of defining the dependent variables in terms of process behavior. The authors refer to possible causal or correlational relations between structural independent variables and process dependent variables as "interact correlates" (p.450). One justification the authors advance for their model is that it provides a framework for more adequately describing the interactional or process effects of certain structural variables on the behavior of small groups over time.

## Structure

The analogue for the Fisher and Hawes model is general systems theory. The structure of the analogue is *grouping*. Its focus is on components on the lowest level of abstraction which, in turn, are combined into even larger groups in yet the next highest level of abstraction.

In the interact model, single acts are grouped to form interacts which, in turn, are grouped to form phases which, in turn, are grouped to form cycles. The cycle is thought of as a system of behavior composed of subsystems of phases. These phases consist of subsystems of interacts. This ability to move up or down levels of abstraction in defining and describing behavior is one of the advantages of using an analogue with a grouping structure. The emphasis of such a structure is on similarities among interconnected subsystems rather than on differences. Grouping structures have holistic rather than reductionistic orientations. The commitment is to put pieces together rather than to take things apart; to identify common attributes rather than to force distinctions.

## Substance

Recall that general systems theory is not a theory in the way we have been using that term. General system theory is a meta-theory; it is a theory about theories rather than an explanation of a particular class of phenomena.

Systems have a structural, functional, and behavioral dimension. The structure of a system is the organization of its component parts at any given moment in time. The structure may change from moment to moment or it may remain relatively constant. The function of a system is its history, development, and change over a period of time. A system may become more complex or it may atrophy. The functional dimension of a system accounts for this history or development over time. The behavior of a system is its particular actions over time. If structure is analogous to a still photograph, behavior is analogous to a motion picture. Observing the behavior of a system for a period of time allows one to operationally describe the function of the system.

Recall that an analogue can be described as having six types of substances; individual choice, collective choice, exchange, adaptation, diffusion, and structure. The *structural* dimension of a system corresponds to structure substance; the function dimension of systems corresponds to *adaptation* substance; and the behavior dimension of a system corresponds to *exchange* substance. Adaptation substance refers to potential change or learning over time. The system adapts to its surrounding environment insofar as the system is open. Exchange substance refers to the behavior dimension insofar as the system exchanges input from the environment with output to the environment. In the process of completing a task, the system is described by utterances exchanged for information, utterances exchanged for utterances, and utterances exchanged for outputs back to the environment in the form of a solution. In doing so, the system, at any point in time, has a particular structure. Over a period of time, that structure has the potential of changing or adapting to new and different circumstances.

## Type

The interact system model is clearly *conceptual*. The authors make no attempt to use mathematical language in describing the model, although it certainly could gain clarity, precision, and specificity if it were stated in mathematical language. Implicit assumptions would be smoked out into the open and vague concepts would have to be defined more precisely or scrapped. Many other investigators using general system theory as the analogue for their models have explicated the models in mathematical language, most notably operation researchers (e.g., Churchman, Ackoff, and Arnoff, 1957).

## Function

The function of the model, as the title of this chapter indicates, is *explicative*. The authors are explicating the concept of "group" in small group interaction theory in a way different from previous definitions of that concept. They are attempting to explicate the concept in terms of behavioral units rather than individual people units.

## Evaluation

The interact model fares better than Becker's or Rosenfield's in terms of the evaluative criteria. The *heuristic* value of the model is relatively clear. The authors have produced a series of studies (e.g., Fisher, 1970a; Fisher 1970b; Hawes, 1972a; Hawes, 1972b; Hawes and Foley, 1973a; Hawes and Foley, 1973b) to answer questions generated by the model.

It is more heuristic than the Westley and MacLean model simply because more is known about the structure and substance of the analogue underlying the Fisher and Hawes model than is known about the same material regarding the Westley and MacLean model.

The interact model meets the *isomorphism* criterion relatively well. Relations among components defined as behaviors can be described as systems as easily as can relations among components defined as individuals. To the extent that relations among components can be measured and defined operationally, systems of behaviors have a structural, functional, and behavioral dimension. To this extent, the structure of the analogue is isomorphic to the substance being mapped onto it.

Fisher and Hawes are specific, to the extent they can be with a conceptual model, in articulating the *rules of correspondence* between the structure of the analogue and the substance being mapped onto it. Each of the three dimensions of a system are defined operationally in terms of communicative behavioral substance. If the model were defined in mathematical rather than natural language, the rules of correspondence would be more particular and less general, enabling other researchers to better test its representational adequacy.

## EXPLICATIVE MODELS: CHOMSKY'S THREE MODELS FOR THE DESCRIPTION OF LANGUAGE

The purpose of the article (Chomsky, 1966, pp.140–152) from which most of this section is drawn is to logically test the adequacy of three different models of language. The three models are, 1) a finite-state Markov process model, 2) a phrase-structure model, and 3) a transformational grammar model.

Chomsky argues that, "The grammar of a language can be viewed as a theory of the structure of this language" (p.141). A grammar, he says, "is based on a finite number of observed sentences (the linguist's corpus) and it 'projects' this set to an infinite set of grammatical sentences by establishing general 'laws' (grammatical rules) framed in terms of such hypothetical constructs as the particular phonemes, words, phrases, and so on, of the language under analysis" (p.141). Chomsky's concern, then, is with the formal structure of a finite set of grammatically correct sentences. He is not concerned with the semantic or logical truth or falsity of the sentences but only with the grammatical or syntactical correctness of a sentence, as judged by a native speaker of the language under consideration.

Before comparing the three models, Chomsky defines language, grammar, and string. *Language* is "a set (finite or infinite) of sentences, each of finite length, all constructed from a finite alphabet of symbols. If A is an alphabet, we shall say that anything formed by concatenating the symbols of A is a *string* in A" (p.142). *Grammar* he defines as, "a device of some sort that produces all of the strings that are sentences of L (language) and only these" (p.142).

With this preliminary work out of the way, Chomsky proceeds to explain three different models that describe language as he defines it. First is the finite-state Markov process model. This model is very similar to the one, described in Chapter 9, used in the Hawes and Foley research on the initial medical interview. The three assumptions of the model are that in determining the present state of the system one only need consider the immediately preceding state, that the system is ergodic, and that the system can occupy only a finite number of states.

Translating these assumptions of the finite-state Markov process model into the language example, the individual rules comprising the grammar of the language correspond to the ergodic source. The grammatical sentences produced by the ergodic source correspond to the states the language system can occupy. If the rules constituting the grammar correspond to sequences of words of a given length, then the grammar will generate a finite number of sentences, some of which are grammatically correct, but also some of which are grammatically incorrect. There is an infinite number of grammatically correct sentences that can be generated by a grammar of the English language. That grammar produces only grammatically correct sentences; the incorrect sentences can be identified as not having been produced by the grammar.

If each rule corresponds to one grammatically correct sentence, there are as many rules as there are grammatically correct sentences. The result is not a grammar that can generate novel, grammatically correct sentences. Consequently, Chomsky rejects the finite-state Markov process as a viable model to represent language.

Chomsky next considers the phrase-structure model. This representation of language conceives of sentences composed of phrases (noun phrases and verb phrases) and phrases being composed of increasingly smaller units until the morphemic units are defined. This is simpler than the finite-state Markov process model insofar as the phrase-structure model consists of logical rules that relate types of phrases into grammatically correct sentences whereas the Markov model statistically relates individual words or arbitrary combinations of words.

However, the phrase-structure model does not provide words for certain grammatically correct sentences nor does it provide rules prohibiting certain grammatically incorrect sentences. For example, the sentence "John is eaten the food" is not prohibited by the rules of a phrase-structure representation of grammar. Clearly, however, that sentence is grammatically incorrect. Phrase-structure models do not have an adequate set of rules to account for passive sentence constructions. Chomsky concludes that appropriate rules for language go beyond the limits of a phrase-structure grammar because an appropriate grammar must account for how sentences, and the constituent elements of sentences, are rearranged so that active sentences can be transformed into passive sentences with appropriate verb form transformations.

A model which does allow for such rearrangements, Chomsky argues, is a transformational grammar model. "Each grammatical transformation T will essentially be a rule that converts every sentence with a given constituent structure into a new sentence with derived constituent structure. The transform and its derived structure must be related in a fixed and constant way to the structure of the transformed string, for each T. We can characterize T by stating, in structural terms, the domain of strings to which it applied and the change it affects on any such string" (p.149).

Chomsky posits the existence of *kernel sentences* which usually are not the actual sentences people use in conversational language. These kernel sentences are derived from terminal strings of phrase-structure grammar via a set of obligatory transformation rules. From these kernel sentences, a wide variety of sentences we use in everyday conversations can be derived by applying various optional transformations on the phrase structures underlying the kernel sentences.

For example, kernel sentences are thought of as a "very small set of simple, active, declarative sentences (probably a finite set of such sentences) such as 'the man ate the food', etc. We then derive questions, passives, sentences with conjunctions, sentences with compound noun phrases (e.g., 'proving that theorem was difficult,' with the NP [noun phrase] 'proving that theorem') etc., by transformations" (p.150). The task confronting researchers using the transformational grammar model is to identify the corpus of kernel sentences and the transformation rules which, when applied to the phrase structure of the string underlying the kernel, result in a wide variety of grammatically correct sentences. Chomsky argues that such an approach has more potential of providing a fundamental understanding of language than the other two models he considers.

## Structure

The structure of the analogue Chomsky uses for his transformational grammar model is a combination of *hierarchical* and *grouping*. The structure is grouping insofar as strings of words are grouped into phrase-structures and these phrase-structures are regrouped into kernel sentences. The analogue is hierarchical insofar as the application of optional transform rules results in a branching of permissable grammatically correct sentences. From a small source, a wide variety of permissable forms of that source are allowed to branch as a result of applying certain rules.

## Substance

The substance of the analogue for Chomsky's model is *structural.* It is structural insofar as any logic is a structural substance. As is apparent from the brief description of the model given above, it is logical rather than empirical in substance. The obligatory and optional transform rules are logical, not empirical, in nature. The result is an inferred logic of language defined by the various rules. The product of the application of rules to a language corpus is a structural description of that language.

## Type

This type of model, like those preceding it, is *conceptual.* Like the preceding authors, Chomsky develops a conceptual vocabulary for representing language. There is no attempt to express the model in an equation form.

## Function

The function of this model, like the function of that of Fisher and Hawes, is *explicative.* Chomsky is not attempting to describe a general process or object. He is trying to more clearly explicate the concept of grammar so that a more adequate description of language might be possible. If his model were a description of language, with all of its component concepts receiving equal attention, the model would have had a more decidedly descriptive function. But Chomsky focuses his attention on the pivotal concept of grammar. Once that concept is explicated, the more general concept of language is viewed differently.

## Evaluation

The model suffers from the limitations of any logically grounded model when the three evaluative criteria are applied. The derivation of new transform rules that account for different grammatically correct sentences is largely up to the intuition and inferential talents of the researcher.

The model certainly is *heuristic*. Since Chomsky formulated it, the transformational grammar model has generated both considerable research and criticism; both responses are excellent indicators of the heuristic value of the model. The *isomorphism* of the model and the material being mapped onto it are the objects of much of the criticism. Do kernel sentences function as the basis for manifested language behavior? How do individuals learn the transform rule? If a native speaker of a language cannot articulate what the rules are, how can they be taught? These are just a few of the questions pertaining to the isomorphic adequacy of the model.

The *rules of correspondence* for the model are as clearly specified as is possible for a logically grounded model. The difficulty is that rules of correspondence frequently are better accounts of rules that already have been devised by the researcher to account for observed language behavior than they are for assisting him in his search for new kernel sentences and their accompanying transform rules.

## FISHBEIN'S MODEL FOR ATTITUDES AND BEHAVIORS

There is a sizable literature on attitude formation, attitude change, and how—indeed *if*—attitudes and behaviors are related. Fishbein (1973) reviews much of the literature pertaining to the attitude-behavior issue and finds that most of the studies conclude that there is little if any relationship between a person's attitude toward an object and his behavior toward that object. The conclusion seems to be that knowing a person's attitude toward a social object does not help us very much in predicting his behavior toward that object.

It has been the purpose of much of Fishbein's research to examine empirically the attitude-behavior theories and to clarify them where possible. In this respect, Fishbein's model has an explicative rather than descriptive *function*. His objective is to explicate more precisely the critical concepts of attitude-behavior theory to facilitate a more sophisticated development of that theory.

Fishbein makes the argument that in most attitude research, attitude is defined as having an affective, cognitive, and conative dimension; yet most operational definitions of attitude have tapped only the affective dimension. Furthermore, the attitudes most frequently used are the intensity of feeling toward some object. For example, subjects frequently are asked to respond on a paper-and-pencil scale how they feel about such objects as Black Panthers, the President, religion, and Jews.

Behaviors, on the other hand, frequently are defined as single behaviors directed toward attitude objects. Fishbein's argument is that affective feelings toward general social objects should not be expected to predict specific individual behaviors. He offers several theoretical and methodological reasons why such an expectation is unrealistic. Rather than redefining the concept of attitude to resolve the difficulty in finding a relation between attitudes and behaviors, Fishbein uses the traditional instrument for operationally defining attitude as an analogue for explicating more precisely the concept of behavior.

He contends that behaviors, like responses on a paper-and-pencil instrument, are data for the social scientist. He quotes McGrath (1964) who defines data as "coded records of selected aspects of behavior" (p.30). This definition includes observed behaviors as well as responses to attitude scales. The methodological irony that Fishbein points out is that although we have relatively rigorous and standardized procedures for constructing and selecting items for an attitude scale, we do not apply similarly rigorous procedures for selecting behaviors to use as the criterion measures of attitude predictors.

Just as there are different types of attitude scale items that can be used as predictors, Fishbein maintains that there are different types of behaviors that can be used as criterion measures for those predictors. He remedies this lack of precision in thinking about the concept of behavior by proposing three basic types of behaviors: single act (i.e., behavior), single observation (i.e., observed and recorded on only one occasion) criteria; single act, repeated observation (i.e., observed and recorded on several different occasions) criteria; and multiple act (i.e., a sequence or group of behaviors observed and counted as the criterion measure for the predictor instrument) criteria (pp.10–11).

After tracing out several theoretical and methodological arguments, Fishbein concludes that it is quite plausible that the traditional definition of attitude (i.e., intensity of affect toward a general social object) should be related to multiple behavior criteria but not to single behavior criteria. The problem is one of properly matching the predictor and what counts as an instance of the criterion.

To this point, Fishbein uses traditional scaling theory and techniques as an analogue, the structure of which serves as an explicative model for the concept of behavior. The result is a finer differentiation of that concept; specifically, three types of behavior rather than one general type.

The second thrust of Fishbein's modeling effort is to explicate the concept of attitude. His argument is that the most parsimonious way of predicting a single behavior criterion is to ask the subject about his intention to perform that particular behavior. The essential consideration in predicting single behavior criterion measures is to match the specificity of the intention to the specificity of the criterion measure. Along this vein, Fishbein contends that there are three considerations that influence the strength of the intentional measure; the time between the measure of intention and the observation of the behavior criterion; and, the degree to which carrying out the intention is under the individual's control (p.15).

To explicate fully the concept of attitude, Fishbein contends that attitude is comprised of two distinct components; the probability that a person assigns to the relation between performing some behavior and that behavior leading to some consequence, and the person's evaluation of that consequence.

With this explicational work completed, Fishbein uses the results of his modeling efforts to construct a more sophisticated theory of the relationship between attitudes and behaviors. The completed theory will not be explored in detail here. Rather, it will be sketched out to provide an idea of how the results of the explicative model are used in building theory.

First, Fishbein stipulates that there is a close correspondence between a particular behavioral criterion and a person's intention to perform that behavior. He casts his theory in mathematical language and explains the relation between behavior (i.e., behavioral intention) and attitude in the form of an equation,

$$B \sim BI = \left[ \sum_{i=1}^{N} B_i a_i \right]_{w_0} + \left[ \sum_{i=1}^{M} NB_i Mc_i \right]_{w_1},$$

where $B$ represents overt behavior; $BI$ represents behavioral intention to perform that behavior; $B_i$ is the belief (i.e., probability or improbability) that performing that behavior will lead to some consequence $i$; $a_i$ is the evaluative aspect of $B_i$, that is, the evaluation of $i$; $N$ represents the number of beliefs; $NB_i$ is the normative belief, that is, the belief that a given other $i$ thinks he should or should not perform the behavior; $Mc_i$ is the motivation to comply with the expectations of $i$; $M$ is the number of relevant others; and $w_0$ and $w_1$ are the regression weights which may take any value.

The first component of the equation is what Fishbein contends is the traditional definition of attitude. But to predict a person's behavior, the theory also posits that we must know a person's normative beliefs pertaining to the behavior and his motivation to comply with the expectations of others. Furthermore, the relation between a person's belief and his evaluation of the outcome (the first component of the equation) and the relation between a person's normative beliefs and his motivation to comply with those beliefs (the second component of the equation) are multiplicative rather than additive.

The point being made by using Fishbein's work as an example is that the theory expressed in mathematical language would not have taken its present form had the pivotal concepts of behavior and attitude not been modeled in an explicative fashion to force out refined distinctions in sharper relief.

### Structure

The structure of the analogue Fishbein uses to model the concepts is *scalar*. He uses the existing methods for operationally defining attitudes, (e.g., Thurstone, Likert, and Guttman scaling procedures) to operationally define behaviors. His contention is that if behaviors are conceived as being scalar structures, then the resulting form of data from attitude and behavior measures are similar. Using a scalar analogue assumes that the data to be mapped onto that structure, thereby forming the model, can be differentiated horizontally in a scale fashion.

### Substance

The substance of Fishbein's analogue is *individual choice*. To draw this conclusion it must be assumed that the individual exercises some degree of choice both over his intention to behave and in actually enacting the behavior observed. The role of the social scientist is to record those individual choices (the intentions and the behaviors) along a horizontally differentiated scale which registers the degree of choice exercised. His objective is to determine the strength of the relation between these two individual choices, and how other intervening conditions influence the nature of that relationship. In this example, such conditions are the concepts represented by the symbols of the equation.

### Evaluation

Fishbein's work rates very well when placed over against the evaluation criteria. The model is extremely *heuristic*. Studies incorporating his definition of behavioral intentions have appeared in communication, social psychology, and sociology journals. There is ample evidence, irrespective of the ultimate worth of the research, that the model has been quite heuristic, at least relative to most of the other models we have considered.

The *isomorphism* of the model is what the resulting theory tests. To what extent can overt behaviors be conceptualized the same way attitudes or behavioral intentions are conceptualized? Do Fishbein's three different types of criterion behaviors actually correspond to different types of items on attitude scale instruments? According to the work of Fishbein and his colleagues (e.g., Ajzen and Fishbein, 1969; Ajzen and Fishbein, 1970), answers to these questions are favorable. Apparently the structure of the analogue and the material being modeled by that structure are quite isomorphic.

Fishbein is very careful to specify the *rules of correspondence* for his model. He spends much time pointing out in what ways overt behaviors can be conceptualized on different levels of specificity just as can attitudes or intentions. His major rule of correspondence is that the specificity of the intention to behave and the actual behavior or behaviors used as criterion measures must be matched in order for the predicted relation between the two classes of phenomena to be observed.

## SIMULATIVE MODEL: HOLDER AND EHLING'S INFORMATION DECISION SIMULATION MODEL

Holder and Ehling (1967, pp.302–315) begin describing their simulation model by maintaining that there are two factors critical to decision-making processes; the way any decision maker (be that an individual or a group) obtains information, and the constraints which available information imposes on the possible alternative outcomes. The reason Holder and Ehling constructed a simulation model was to investigate the dynamic influence of information on outcome probability over time (i.e., during the decisioning process). "The purpose of this paper is to report on efforts to construct a formal information decision model which attempts to take into account the interrelationship of information selection and decision making and to treat this interrelationship dynamically" (p.303).

The assumption underlying the model is relatively simple and straightforward; "Each time any decision alternative open to a decision maker is reinforced by information with which the decision maker comes in contact, the probability that this alternative will be selected by a decision maker is increased" (p.304). To operationalize this assumption, the authors use a theory of Markov chains as the analogue. As you recall from the discussion of the Hawes and Foley (1973) work, Markov chains represent types of behaviors as states and these behavioral states have a certain probability of making a transition to another behavioral state. The matrix that represents the probabilities of all possible one-step transitions is called the transition probability matrix. In the Hawes and Foley research, the assumption of an ergodic source was being tested. Holder and Ehling in their model make the assumption that the elements of the transition matrix do change over time. Specifically, they want to determine how the introduction of different types of information influences the probability of any given alternative being selected as the final decision.

For Holder and Ehling, the elements of the transition matrix are the alternative outcomes. Each outcome is assigned an initial probability of being selected. Pieces of information are then introduced which are relevant to selecting an outcome, and the changes in the cell values of the transition probability matrix are observed. The authors programmed a rule which stated, in general terms, that if one alternative element in the transition probability matrix was reinforced by being presented with a piece of information reinforcing that alternative, the probability of the other alternatives being selected will decrease by a fixed power.

The critical assumption the authors are making is that human communication behaves in a Markov-like way. They argue that their model has two advantages over traditional communication models. First, the Markov model is based on transition probabilities that specify the movement from one state to another and therefore take into account behavior changes over time. Second, the Markov process is more isomorphic to actual communication processes and does not merely test for degree of association between independent and dependent variables as is represented by most other models.

The rationale for the model is that to study the dynamic properties of decision making the process must be simulated rather than simply observed for static relationships among variables. The model is an attempt to represent a process that changes over time. In order to obtain the advantages of simulating a dynamic process, certain simplifying assumptions have to be made. For example, Holder and Ehling assume that there are only two alternative outcomes and that when information is read into the program that reinforces one alternative, the probability of the other alternative is reduced by a factor of two. Nevertheless, even after making such simplifying assumptions, Holder and Ehling obtain some very interesting data.

Six conclusions are identified. First, the earlier a decision maker obtains a piece of information that reinforces a particular alternative, the more impact that information input has on the decisioning process. Second, the smaller the probability of any alternative being selected, the more that probability is weakened when information inputs challenge it. Third, the more the decisioning process converges toward the selection of one alternative, the more difficult it is for competing information inputs to halt the convergence. Fourth, the impact of any one information input is related to the number of other inputs which reinforce the same alternative over a series of reconsiderations. Fifth, drastic changes in the transition probability matrix and extreme shifts of preference do not occur through the influence of one or two information inputs; change is gradual and without sudden jumps in transition probabilities. Finally, the communication contact which eventually pushes the transition matrix into a final decision or absorbing state actually makes very little change in the probabilities of the transition matrix.

## Structure

The structure of the Markov chain theory that Holder and Ehling use as their analogue is *spatio-temporal*. This is one of the advantages the authors claim for their simulation model, and one of the identifying characteristics of simulation models in general. They represent a process as it changes in space and over time. This is what gives the simulation model its dynamic character.

## Substance

The substance of the Holder and Ehling analogue is a combination of *exchange, adaptation,* and *structure.* Recall the discussion of the substance of the analogue Fisher and Hawes (1971) use in their interact system model. They rely on a Markov chain theory as an analogue for their model also. The substance is exchange insofar as it represents the behavior dimension of a system. The behavior dimension represents the exchange of behaviors that define the structure of the process at any given point in time. Recall that a process can change from moment to moment or it can remain relatively stable over a long period of time. But whether a process changes its structure from moment to moment or remains stable, the process is behavior being enacted. When that behavior is frozen in time, the static picture of the process is a representation of the structure.

The adaptation dimension of the substance of the information decision analogue represents the history, development, or evolution of the process over time. If the change in probability associated with one particular decision outcome over the course of the decisioning process if profiled, a representation of the adaptation or function dimension of the process is obtained.

## Type

The information decision model is *mathematical* to the extent that it relies on a mathematical theory as its analogue. Dimensions of the material being modeled are treated as mathematical parameters and assigned numerical values. The values of these parameters are changed to determine the resultant effects on the process over time. For example, the authors varied the initial probability values assigned to the two alternative outcomes to determine the influence of information inputs on the resulting probability values for those alternatives.

## Evaluation

Considering the evaluative criteria, not much can be said about the actual *heuristic* value of Holder and Ehling's candidate. It is difficult to determine how much research this particular model has generated. It must be admitted that Markov chain theories, used as analogues for models, have been used heuristically in the social sciences. Probably the most systematic use of that type of model is by Suppes and Atkinson (1960) in their research on learning. The potential heuristic value of this particular model is most promising, if based only on the past performance of these types of models in general.

There is some question as to the *isomorphism* criterion being satisfied by Markov chain models. The real questions involve the degree of restrictedness imposed on the model by the necessary mathematical assumptions. One such assumption is that the state of a system at any point in time is determined only by the state that system was in during the immediately preceding time period. The assumption of ergodic sources can be circumvented, as Holder and Ehling did in their work. The probabilities assigned to behavioral states are assumed to change over time and the model is designed accordingly.

The *rules of correspondence* are stipulated clearly. Especially in the construction of a computer simulation model, to write the program to drive the model, all parameters of the substance being modeled by the program must be specified or the program will not function. In addition, these critical parameters must be given a value so that the value of other concepts can be observed and measured over time. In short, the Holder and Ehling model fares quite well, relative to the other models considered in this chapter.

## CONCLUSION

For it is necessary to insist upon this extraordinary but undeniable fact; experimental science has progressed thanks in great part to the work of men astonishingly mediocre, and even less than mediocre. . . . The reason of this lies in what is at the same time the great advantage and the gravest peril of the new science . . . namely, mechanization. . . . For the purpose of innumerable investigations it is possible to divide science into small sections, to enclose oneself in one of these, and to leave out of consideration all the rest. The solidity and exactitude of methods allow of this temporary but quite real disarticulation of knowledge. The work is done under one of these methods as with a machine, and in order to obtain quite abundant results, it is not even necessary to have rigorous notions of their meaning and foundations.

In certain respects, José Ortega y Gasset's observation in *The Revolt of the Masses* holds true for much of the research in communication we call social scientific. This admission, however, is not to conclude that Gasset's description of doing science must apply necessarily. One of the most exhilirating, and at the same time sobering, experiences is to be caught up in the freedom to explore uncharted intellectual territory. Our study of human communication is limited only by our lack of ingenuity and imagination. To retreat totally to the safety of mechanization is to do science in its crudest and most unimaginative form. To equate science with mechanization is to misunderstand the fundamental nature of the activity.

Johan Huizinga (1950), in his delightful book *Homo Ludens*, contends that among other things, man is a playing and playful animal. Doing science, he would agree, is a form of adult play; theories and models are adult toys. Not to dare to play intellectually is to preclude the possibility of doing original social science at all. But intellectual play must be a rigorous exercise to avoid degenerating into chaos. This book was intended to provide some intellectual tools to make the activity less than chaotic motion but more than mediocre mechanization.

# References

Abelson, R. P., E. Aronson, W. J. McGuire, T. M. Newcomb, M. J. Rosenberg, and P. H. Tannenbaum (eds.), (1968). *Theories of Cognitive Consistency: A Sourcebook.* Chicago: Rand McNally

Abelson, R. P., and A. Bernstein, (1963). A computer simulation model of community referendum controversies. *Public Opinion Quarterly* **27,** pp.93–192.

Adler, A. (1935). The fundamental views of individual psychogy. *International Journal of Individual Psychology,* **1,** pp.5–8.

Ajzen, I., and M. Fishbein (1969). The prediction of behavioral intentions in a choice situation. *Journal of Experimental Social Psychology,* **5,** pp.400–416.

Ajzen, I., and M. Fishbein (1970). The prediction of behavior from attitudinal and normative variables. *Journal of Experimental Social Psychology,* **6,** pp.466–487.

Aldrich, V. C. (1963). *Philosophy of Art.* Englewood Cliffs, N.J.: Prentice-Hall.

Bales, R. F. (1950). *Interaction Process Analysis.* Reading, Mass.: Addison-Wesley.

Bales, R. F. (1970). *Personality and Interpersonal Behavior.* New York: Holt, Rinehart and Winston.

Bandura, A. (1969). *Principles of Behavior Modification.* New York: Holt, Rinehart and Winston.

Barker, R. G. (1968). *Ecological Psychology.* Stanford, Calif.: Stanford University Press.

Barnlund, D. C. (1968). *Interpersonal Communication: Survey and Studies.* Boston: Houghton Mifflin.

Bates, A. P., and J. S. Cloyd (1956). Toward the development of operations for defining group norms and member roles. *Sociometry,* **19,** pp.26–39.

Becker, S. L. (1968). Toward an appropriate theory for contemporary speech-communication. In D. H. Smith (ed.), *What Rhetoric (Communication Theory) Is Appropriate for Contemporary Speech Communication?* The Proceedings of the University of Minnesota Spring Symposium in Speech-Communication, pp.9–25.

Berger, J., B. P. Cohen, J. L. Snell, and M. Zelditch, Jr. (1962). *Types of Formalization in Small Group Research.* Boston: Houghton Mifflin.

Berlo, D. K. (1960). *The Process of Communication.* New York: Holt, Rinehart and Winston.

Biddle, B. J., and E. J. Thomas (eds.), (1966). *Role Theory: Concepts and Research.* New York: John Wiley & Sons.

Black, E. B. (1965). *Rhetorical Criticism: A Study in Method.* New York: Macmillan.

Black, M. (1962). *Models and Metaphors.* Ithaca, N.Y.: Cornell University Press.

Blalock, H. M. Jr. (1969). *Theory Construction.* Englewood Cliffs, N.J.: Prentice-Hall.

Blau, P. M. (1964). *Exchange and Power in Social Life.* New York: John Wiley & Sons.

Bormann, E. G. (1970). The paradox and promise of small group research. *Speech Monographs,* **37,** 211–215.

Brehm, J. W., and A. R. Cohen (1962). *Explorations in Cognitive Dissonance.* New York: John Wiley & Sons.

Brodbeck, M. (ed.), (1968). *Readings in the Philosophy of the Social Sciences.* New York: Macmillan.

Bronowski, J. (1965). *The Identity of Man.* Garden City, N.Y.: The Natural History Press.

Bronowski, J. (1965). *Science and Human Values.* New York: Harper & Row.

Brown, R. (1963). *Explanation in Social Science.* Chicago: Aldine.

Buck, R. C. (1956). On the logic of general behavior systems theory. In H. Feigl and M. Scriven (eds.), *Minnesota Studies in the Philosophy of Science,* vol. I. Minneapolis: University of Minnesota Press.

Bunge, M. (1970). Analogy, simulation, representation. *General Systems* **15,** 27–34.

Burke, K. (1941). *The Philosophy of Literary Form.* Baton Rouge, La.: Louisiana State University Press.

Burke, K. (1945). *A Grammar of Motives.* Englewood Cliffs, N.J.: Prentice-Hall.

Burke, K. (c1950). *A Rhetoric of Motives.* New York: George Braziller.

Burke, K. (1952). A dramatistic view of the origins of language, part I. *The Quarterly Journal of Speech* **38,** 251–264.

Burke, K. (1953). *Counter-statement.* 2nd ed., rev. Los Altos, Calif.: Hermes.

Burke, K. (1954). *Permanence and Change.* 2nd ed., rev. Los Altos, Calif.: Hermes.

Campbell, N. R. (1920). *Physics, the Elements.* Cambridge: University Press

Campbell, P. N. (1972). *Rhetoric Ritual.* Belmont, Calif.: Dickenson.

Cantril, H. (1965). *The Pattern of Human Concerns.* New Brunswick, N.J.: Rutgers University.

Cartwright, D., and F. Harary (1956). Structural balance: a generalization of Heider's theory. *Psychological Review* **63,** pp.277–293.

Catanese, A. J., and A. W. Steiss (1970). *Systemic Planning: Theory and Application.* Lexington, Mass.: D. C. Heath.

Chomsky, N. (1964). *Current Issues in Linguistic Theory.* The Hague: Mouton.

Chomsky, N. (1965). *Aspects of the Theory of Syntax.* Cambridge, Mass.: M.I.T. Press.

Chomsky, N. (1966). Three models for the description of language. In A. J. Smith (ed.), *Communication and Culture.* New York: Holt, Rinehart and Winston.

Churchman, C. W., R. L. Ackoff, and E. L. Arnoff (1957). *Introduction to Operations Research.* New York: Wiley.

Cohen, A. R. (1964). *Attitude Change and Social Influence.* New York: Basic Books.

Coleman, J. S. (1973). *The Mathematics of Collective Action.* Chicago: Aldine.

Collins, B. E., and H. Guetzkow (1964): *A Social Psychology of Group Process for Decision-making.* New York: Wiley.

Crow, W. J. (1967). *The Role of Simulation-model Construction in Social Research on Post-nuclear Attack Events.* La Jolla, Calif.: Western Behavioral Sciences Institute.

Davis, M. D. (1970). *Game Theory.* New York: Basic Books.

Deese, J. (1969). Conceptual categories in the study of content. In G. Gerbner, O. R. Holsti, K. Krippendorff, W. J. Paisley, and P. J. Stone (eds.), *The Analysis of Communication Content.* New York: Wiley.

Deutsch, K. E. (1963). *The Nerves of Government.* New York: The Free Press.

Drabek, T. E. (1969). *Laboratory Simulation of a Police Communications System under Stress.* Columbus, Ohio: College of Administrative Science.

Dubin, R. (1969). *Theory Building.* New York: The Free Press.

Dumont, M. (1969). *The Absurd Healer.* New York: Science House.

Duncan, H. D. (1962). *Communication and Social Order.* London: Oxford University Press.

Duncan, H. D. (1968). *Symbols in Society.* London: Oxford University Press.

Dunphy, D. C. (1972). *The Primary Group: A Handbook for Analysis and Field Research.* New York: Appleton-Century-Crofts.

Durkheim, E. (1933). *The Division of Labor in Society.* Trans. by G. Simpson. Glencoe, Ill.: The Free Press.

Edwards, W., and A. Tversky (1967). *Decision Making.* New York: Penguin Books.

Feinberg, G. (1968). *The Prometheus Project.* Garden City, N.Y.: Doubleday.

Fishbein, M. (ed.), (1967). *Reading in Attitude Theory and Measurement.* New York: John Wiley & Sons.

Fishbein, M. (1973). The prediction of behaviors from attitudinal variables. In C. D. Mortensen and K. K. Sereno (eds.), *Advances in Communication Research.* New York: Harper & Row.

Fisher, B. A. (1970a). Decision emergence: phases in group decision making." *Speech Monographs,* **37,** pp.53–66.

Fisher, B. A. (1970b). The process of decision modification in small discussion groups. *The Journal of Communication,* **20,** pp.51–64.

Fisher, B. A., and L. C. Hawes (1971). An interact system model: generating a grounded theory of small groups. *The Quarterly Journal of Speech* **57,** pp.444–453.

Fogarty, D. (1959), *Roots for a New Rhetoric.* New York: Russell & Russell.

Freud, S. (1949). *An Outline of Psychoanalysis.* New York: W. W. Norton.

Freud, S. (1953). *The Standard Edition of the Complete Psychological Works of Sigmund Freud.* Trans. by J. Strachey. London: Hogarth.

Gagné, R. M. (1962). *Psychological Principles in System Development.* New York: Holt, Rinehart and Winston.

Garfinkel, H. (1964). Studies of the routine grounds of everyday activities. *Social Problems* **11,** pp.225–250.

Garfinkel, H. (1967). *Studies in Ethnomethodology.* Englewood Cliffs, N.J.: Prentice-Hall.

Gergen, K. J. (1969). *The Psychology of Behavior Exchange.* Reading, Mass.: Addison-Wesley.

Gibbs, J. P. (1967). Identification of statements in theory construction. *Sociology and Social Research* **52,** pp.72–87.

Goffman, E. (1959). *The Presentation of Self in Everyday Life.* Garden City, N.Y.: Doubleday.

Goffman, E. (1963). *Behavior in Public Places.* New York: The Free Press.

Goffman, E. (1969). *Strategic Interaction.* Philadelphia: University of Pennsylvania Press.

Goslin, D. A. (ed.), (1969). *Handbook of Socialization Theory and Research.* Chicago: Rand McNally.

Gouldner, A. W. (1960). The norm of reciprocity: a preliminary statement. *American Sociological Review* **25,** pp.161–178.

Gouran, D. E. (1970). Response to "the paradox and promise of small group research." *Speech Monographs* **37,** pp.216–218.

Greer, S. (1969). *The Logic of Social Inquiry.* Chicago: Aldine.

Grier, W., and P. Cobbs (1968). *Black Rage.* New York: Basic Books.

Guetzkow, H. (1970). A decade of life with inter-nation simulation. In R. M. Stogdill (ed.), *The Process of Model-building in the Behavioral Sciences.* Columbus, Ohio: Ohio State University Press.

Gullahorn, J. T., and J. E. Gullahorn (1963). A computer model of elementary social behavior. *Behavioral Science* **8,** pp.354–362.

Handy, R. (1964). *Methodology of the Behavioral Sciences.* Springfield, Ill.: Charles C. Thomas.

Hawes, L. C. (1972a). Development and application of an interview coding system. *Central States Speech Journal* **23,** pp.92–99.

Hawes, L. C. (1972b). The effects of interviewer style on patterns of dyadic communication. *Speech Monographs* **39,** pp.114–123.

Hawes, L. C. (1973). *The Analysis of Decision-making in Small Groups.* Final Project Report to U.S. Department of Health, Education, and Welfare. Grant # OEG–0–72–4520.

Hawes, L. C., and J. M. Foley (1973). A Markov analysis of interview communication. *Speech Monographs* **40,** pp.208–219.

Heider, F. (1944). Social perception and phenomenal causality. *Psychological Review* **51,** pp.358–374.

Heider, F. (1946). Attitudes and cognitive organization. *Journal of Psychology* **21,** pp.107–112.

Heider, F. (1958). *The Psychology of Interpersonal Relations.* New York: Wiley.

Hesse, M. B. (1966). *Models and Analogies in Science.* Notre Dame, Indiana: University of Notre Dame Press.

Hofling, C. K. (1967). *Basic Psychiatric Concepts in Nursing.* Philadelphia: J. B. Lippincott.

Holder, H. D., and W. P. Ehling (1967). Construction and simulation of an information decision model. *Journal of Communication* **17,** pp.302–315.

Homans, G. C. (1961). *Social Behavior: Its Elementary Forms.* New York: Harcourt, Brace, and World.

Huizinga, J. (1950). *Homo Ludens.* Boston: Beacon Press.

Insko, C. A. (1967). *Theories of Attitude Change.* New York: Appleton-Century-Crofts.

Jung, C. G. (1950). *Shadow, Animus, and Anima.* New York: Analytic Psychology Club.

Kahn, R. L., D. M. Wolfe, R. P. Quinn, and J. D. Snoek (1964). *Organizational Stress: Studies in Role Conflict and Ambiguity.* New York: Wiley.

Kaplan, A. (1964). *The Conduct of Inquiry.* San Francisco: Chandler.

Katz, E. (1957). The two-step flow of communication: an up-to-date report on an hypothesis. *Public Opinion Quarterly* **21,** pp.61–78.

Katz, E. (1961). The social itinerary of technical change: two studies on the diffusion of innovation. *Human Organization* **20,** pp.70–82.

Katz, E., and P. F. Lazarsfeld (1955). *Personal Influence: The Part Played by People in the Flow of Mass Communications.* Glencoe, Ill.: The Free Press.

Kemeny, J. G., and J. L. Snell (1960). *Finite Markov Chains.* New York: D. Van Nostrand.

Kemeny, J. G., and J. L. Snell (1962). *Mathematical Models in the Social Sciences.* Cambridge, Mass.: The M.I.T. Press.

Kerckhoff, A. C. (1970). A theory of hysterical contagion. In T. Shibutani (ed.), *Human Nature and Collective Behavior.* Englewood Cliffs, N.J.: Prentice-Hall.

Kuhn, M. (1964). Major trends in symbolic interaction theory in the past twenty-five years. *The Sociological Quarterly* **5,** pp.61–84.

Kuhn, T. S. (1970). *The Structure of Scientific Revolutions.* 2nd ed. Chicago: University of Chicago Press.

Kyburg, Jr., H. E. (1968). *Philosophy of Science: A Formal Approach.* New York: Macmillan.

Labov, W. (1966). *The Social Stratification of English in New York City.* Washington, D.C.: Center for Applied Linguistics.

Lang, K., and G. E. Lang (1970). Collective behavior theory and the escalated riots of the sixties. In T. Shibutani (ed.), *Human Nature and Collective Behavior.* Englewood Cliffs, N.J.: Prentice-Hall.

Lazarsfeld, P. F. (1969). *Mathematical Thinking in the Social Sciences.* New York: Russell & Russell.

Levi-Strauss, C. (1969). *The Raw and the Cooked.* New York: Harper & Row.

Lieberman, M. A., I. D. Yalom, and M. B. Miles (1973). *Encounter Groups: First Facts.* New York: Basic Books.

Macaulay, I., and L. Berkowitz (eds.), (1970). *Altruism and Helping Behavior.* New York: Academic Press.

Maier, N. R. F. (1963). *Problem-solving Discussions and Conferences: Leadership Method and Skills.* New York: McGraw Hill.

Maier, N. R. F., and H. W. Reninger (1933). *A Psychological Approach to Literary Criticism.* Folcroft, Pa.: Folcroft.

Malinowski, B. (1948). *Magic, Science and Religion, and Other Essays.* Glencoe, Ill.: The Free Press.

March, J. G. (1970). Making artists out of pedants. In R. M. Stogdill (ed.), *The Process of Model-building in the Behavioral Sciences.* Columbus, Ohio: Ohio State University Press.

Maruyama, M. (1963). The second cybernetics: deviation-amplifying mutual causal processes. *American Scientist* **51**, pp.164–179.

McGrath, J. E. (1964). *Social Psychology.* New York: Holt, Rinehart and Winston.

McGrath, J. E., and I. Altman (1966). *Small Group Research: A Synthesis and Critique of the Field.* New York: Holt, Rinehart and Winston.

Miller, G. R. (1973). Counterattitudinal advocacy: a current appraisal. In C. D. Mortensen and K. K. Sereno (eds.), *Advances in Communication Research.* New York: Harper & Row.

Miller, J. G. (1965). Living systems: basic concepts. *Behavioral Science* **10**, pp.193–237, 337–411.

Mills, C. W. (1959). *The Sociological Imagination.* London: Oxford University Press.

Monge, P. R. (1973). Theory construction in the study of communication: the system paradigm. *The Journal of Communication* **23**, pp.5–16.

Mortensen, C. D., and K. K. Sereno (1970). The influence of ego-involvement and discrepancy of perception on communication. *Speech Monographs* **37**, pp.127–134.

Newcomb, T. M. (1953). "An approach to the study of communicative acts." *Psychological Review* **60**, pp.393–404.

Parsons, T. (1937). *The Structure of Social Action.* New York: The Free Press.

Pearson, K. (1969). *The Grammar of Science.* Gloucester, Mass.: Peter Smith.

Pierce, J. R. (1961). *Symbols, Signals, and Noise.* New York: Harper & Row.

Polanyi, M. (1946). *Science, Faith, and Society.* Chicago: The University of Chicago Press.

Polanyi, M. (1958). *Personal Knowledge.* New York: Harper Torchbooks.

Polanyi, M. (1959). *The Study of Man.* Chicago: The University of Chicago Press.

Radcliff-Brown, A. R. (1924). The mother's brother in South Africa. *South African Journal of Science* **21,** pp.542–555.

Radcliff-Brown, A. R. (1949). A further note on joking relationships. *Africa* **19,** pp.133–140.

Raser, J. R. (1969). *Simulation and Society.* Boston: Allyn and Bacon.

Richards, I. A. (1936). *The Philosophy of Rhetoric.* Oxford: Oxford University Press.

Rogers, E. M. (1962). *Diffusion of Innovations.* New York: The Free Press.

Rogers, E. M. (1969). *Modernization among Peasants.* New York: Holt, Rinehart and Winston.

Rogers, E. M., and F. F. Shoemaker (1971). *Communication of Innovations.* New York: The Free Press.

Rosenfield, L. W. (1968). A game model of human communication. In D. H. Smith (ed.), *What Rhetoric (Communication Theory) Is Appropriate for Contemporary Speech Communication?* The Proceedings of the University of Minnesota Spring Symposium in Speech-communication, pp.26–41.

de Santillana, G. (1941). Aspects of scientific rationalism in the nineteenth-century. *International Encyclopedia of Unified Science.* Chicago: University of Chicago Press, Vol. 2, p.7.

Sereno, K. K. (1968). Ego-involvement, high source credibility, and response to a belief discrepant communication. *Speech Monographs* **35,** pp.476–481.

Sereno, K. K. (1969). "Ego-involvement: a neglected variable in speech-communication." *Quarterly Journal of Speech* **55,** pp.69–77.

Sereno, K. K., and E. Bodaken (1972). Ego-involvement and attitude change: toward a reconceptualization of persuasive effect. *Speech Monographs* **39,** pp.151–158.

Sereno, K. K., and C. D. Mortensen (1969). The effects of ego-involved attitudes on conflict negotiation in dyads. *Speech Monographs* **36,** pp.8–12.

Shannon, C. E., and W. Weaver (1964). *The Mathematical Theory of Communication.* Urbana, Ill.: University of Illinois Press.

Sherif, M., O. J. Harvey, B. J. White, W. R. Hood, and C. G. Sherif (1961). *Intergroup Conflict and Cooperation: the Robber's Cave Experiment.* Norman, Okla.: University of Oklahoma Press.

Sherif, C. W. and M. Sherif (1967). *Attitude, Ego-involvement and Change.* New York: Wiley.

Sherif, C. W., M. Sherif, and R. E. Nebergall (1965). *Attitude and Attitude Change: The Social Judgement-involvement Approach.* Philadelphia: W. B. Saunders.

Shibutani, T. (1966). *Improvised News*. Indianapolis: Bobbs-Merrill.

Sudnow, D. (Ed.), (1972). *Studies in Social Interaction*. New York: The Free Press.

Suppes, P., and R. C. Atkinson (1960). *Markov Learning Models for Multiperson Interactions*. Stanford: Stanford University Press.

Tarde, G. (1969). *On Communication and Social Influence*. T. N. Clark, (ed.). Chicago: University of Chicago Press.

Taylor, D. M. (1970). *Explanation and Meaning*. Cambridge: Cambridge University Press.

Theodorson, G. A. (ed.), (1961). *Studies in Human Ecology*. New York: Harper & Row.

Thonssen, L., and A. C. Baird (1948). *Speech Criticism*. New York: The Ronald Press.

Toulmin, S. (1969). Concepts and the Explanation of Human Behavior. In Mischel, T. (ed.), *Human Action*. New York: Academic Press, pp.71–104.

Walton, R. E., and R. B. McKersie (1965). *A Behavioral Theory of Labor Negotiations*. New York: McGraw-Hill.

Watts, A. W. (1967). *The Book*. New York: Macmillan.

Watzlawick, P., J. H. Beavin, and D. D. Jackson (1967). *Pragmatics of Human Communication*. New York: W. W. Norton.

Weaver, R. (1953). *The Ethics of Rhetoric*. Chicago: Gateway.

Weaver, W. (1964). The imperfections of science. In S. Rapport and H. Wright, (eds.), *Science: Method and Meaning*. New York: Washington Square Press.

Westley, B. H., and M. S. MacLean, Jr. (1965). "A conceptual model for communications research. In James H. Campbell and Hal W. Hepler (eds.), *Dimensions in Communication*. Belmont, Calif.: Wadsworth.

Wiener, N. (1967). *The Human Use of Human Beings*. New York: Avon.

Zetterberg, H. L. (1966). *On Theory and Verification in Sociology*. Totowa, N.J.: Bedminister Press.

# Author Index

# Subject Index